SO-BNH-883

Cambodian for Beginners

WITHDRAWN

by
Richard K. Gilbert

(រិឆាត យ. គិលប៊ីត)

Sovandy Hang

(ហង្ស សុវណ្ណឌី)

PAIBOON
PUBLISHING

ភាសាខ្មែរ

Cambodian for Beginners
Copyright ©2004 by Paiboon Publishing

Printed in Thailand
All rights reserved

Paiboon Poomsan Publishing
582 Amarinniwate Village 2
Nawamin 90 (Sukha 1), Bungkum
Bangkok 10230
THAILAND
Tel   662-509-8632
Fax 662-519-5437

info@paiboonpublishing.com
www.paiboonpublishing.com

Paiboon Publishing
PMB 192, 1442A Walnut Street
Berkeley, California USA 94709
Tel. 1-510-848-7086
Fax 1-510-848-4521

info@paiboonpublishing.com
www.paiboonpublishing.com

Cover picture: Neary Hang
Cover and graphic design by Randy Kincaid
Edited by Ron Colvin II and Benjawan Poomsan Becker
Transliterations: Paiboon Publishing

ISBN 1-887521-35-6

Printed by Chulalongkorn University Printing House
Tel. 0-2218-3563, 0-2215-3612   November 2006
[5002-079/1,500(2)]
http://www.cuprint.chula.ac.th

Introduction

Jum-riab-sua! Hello!

Welcome to the kingdom and the language of Cambodia, one of Asia's most exotic lands and cultures. Today, many people are eager to learn the Cambodian language, officially known as Khmer, but until now there was no effective textbook to show them the way. This book solves the problem.

Cambodian for Beginners is easy to use and easy to understand. It teaches the four basic language skills: speaking, listening (with the compact discs), reading, and writing. The first part of each lesson teaches vocabulary and sentence structure. As a helpful tool, a vocabulary list with Cambodian spelling, transliteration, and English definitions appears at the beginning of each chapter.

The second part of each lesson teaches students how to read and write. At first glance, the Cambodian script looks exotic and difficult to understand, and many students wonder if it is worth the trouble. Their primary goal is to learn how to hold an effective conversation, so why go to all the trouble of learning the alphabet? Through these lessons, though, students quickly discover that learning the script is much easier than it looks. Written Cambodian uses no spaces between words. But we do put spaces in, so that beginning students can master the script more easily. Students also quickly discover that learning the Cambodian alphabet is indeed worth the trouble. Because the written language is almost entirely phonetic, learning the alphabet greatly facilitates pronunciation and comprehension. So we begin teaching the Cambodian alphabet from the very first lesson.

The book includes three appendixes with important learning tools. The first appendix helps students plunge right into using the language: it lists many common Cambodian phrases that students can use to make conversation with Cambodians or to use in their travels. The second contains an introduction and summary of the Cambodian alphabet. And the third gives the answers to the drills and quizzes that are set forth in each chapter.

Although this book is designed for beginners, it is also an ideal tool for people who want to improve their basic skills in Cambodian and build a foundation for future studies. It is also very useful for individuals preparing a trip to Cambodia. The book can be used either for individual study or as a formal classroom textbook.

The Cambodian language differs from English in many ways. Here are the basics:

❑   Adjectives follow the noun.
In Cambodian we say "dog big" (chgae tom) instead of "big dog."

❑   There are no verb conjugations in Cambodian. Even though there are official ways to classify tenses, they are not commonly used in practice. Tenses are understood from the context of the sentence or from other identifying words that indicate time.

❑   There are no articles (a, an, the)

❑   There is no "to be" verb used with adjectives.
"He is skinny" would be "He skinny." (goat sgoom)

❑   Written Cambodian is almost 100 percent phonetic.

Even though Cambodia is a somewhat obscure country, the Cambodian language is increasingly in demand. Now that Cambodia has overcome its recent history of war, it is once again open to the outside world. Foreign investment and economic development have begun to take hold in Cambodia, and the Angkor Wat temples have become a world-renowned tourist attraction. Foreign countries such as the United States also have large populations of Cambodian speakers. However, there are still very few individuals who have actually been able to learn the Cambodian language. This book will help those individuals overcome this language barrier in order to more fully enjoy Cambodia and its people.

Note on Transliteration

The transliteration system is designed to provide students with an introduction to Cambodian pronunciation. Every effort was taken to create a phonetically correct transliteration system. However, the system is not perfect because many sounds in the Cambodian language do not exist in English and cannot be properly represented phonetically. Therefore, it is imperative that the student begins his or her study of Cambodian with the help of the accompanying cassette tapes or a competent teacher.

Even though it is important to thoroughly understand the transliteration system in this book, the system should be considered nothing more than a crutch. No one in Cambodia has ever seen or heard of such a transliteration system. It should be discarded as soon as possible and replaced with the Cambodian alphabet.

Table of Contents

Guide to Pronunciation

Sounds

While Cambodian is not a tonal language, it does have its challenges. The hardest part is learning proper pronunciation. This can be especially difficult for English speakers because there are many sounds in Cambodian that are not represented in the English language. Also, there are many subtleties to master. If you pronounce a word or a phrase incorrectly, other people may not understand what you mean to say. But here is the good news: our transliteration script will help you immensely, as you will see below. We cannot possibly provide a fully accurate phonetic reflection of each language sound, so students should use the compact discs for this book or a competent teacher when learning these sounds for the first time.

Vowels

Cambodian vowels can be short or long, and each vowel can have two sounds depending on the consonant used. Short vowels are clipped and cut off at the end. Long ones are drawn out. This book shows short vowels with a single letter and long vowels with double letters ("a" for short; "aa" for long).

Many of these vowel sounds have no comparable sound in English. While it is possible to find English words with vowels that are somewhat similar to the Cambodian vowel, the sound is not exactly the same. For this reason, it is imperative that the student uses the compact discs as a study aid to develop correct pronunciation. Vowels and consonants with little or no English equivalent are marked with an asterisk.

Simple Vowels

ɔ	like ɔ in <u>o</u>pportunity	jɔng - to want
ɔɔ	like ɔɔ in <u>Au</u>gust	dɔɔb - bottle
a	like <u>a</u> in apple	gat - to cut
aa	like <u>a</u> in c<u>a</u>t	dtaa - grandfather
i	like <u>i</u> in t<u>i</u>p	jit - close
e	like <u>e</u> in b<u>e</u>t	jet - heart
ii	like <u>ee</u> in s<u>ee</u>	dtii - place
ey	like <u>ey</u> in h<u>ey</u>	dey - land *
ə	like <u>ə</u> in g<u>u</u>n	dəng - to know
əə	like <u>əə</u> in teach<u>er</u> without the r sound	jəəng - foot, leg *
ʉʉ	like <u>ʉʉ</u> in r<u>u</u>ler	gʉʉ - is, to be *
o	like <u>o</u> in n<u>o</u>te	dtok - table
oo	like <u>ow</u> in sh<u>ow</u>	goon - child
u	like <u>u</u> in fl<u>u</u>te	dtuk - to keep
uu	like <u>oo</u> in s<u>oo</u>n	juun - to send
ee	like <u>a</u> in l<u>a</u>te	deek - to sleep
ɛɛ	similar to ee (not common)	mɛɛn - real *

Complex Vowels

The following dipthongs are combinations of the above vowels.

au	gaʉt - to be born	ao	gao - to shave
ia	rian - to study	ua	suan- park
ʉa	jʉa - to believe	ae	daek - metal
ai	dai - hand	ei	prei - forest
au	jau - grandchildren	əʉ	nəʉ - at, present
oa	groan - better	ɛa	lɛak - to hide

Consonant Combination Vowels

The following vowels have a final consonant sound.

om	gom - "don't"	um	bprɔ-jum - meeting
ɔm	jɔm - exactly	am	jam - to remember
oam	noam - to lead	eh	beh - to pick, pluck
ih	nih - this	oh	joh - to descend
uh	pdtuh - to explode	ɔh	gch - island
ang	dtang - to appoint	ɛang	rɛang - dry, lack of rain
ɛah	dtɛah - to slap	uah	bpruah - because
əm	rəm-pəəb - excited	ah	bah - to touch

Consonants

g	as in gold	gat - to cut
k	as in kiss	kam - to bite
ng	as in ringing	ngiay - easy
j	as in jet	jeek - banana *
ch	as in chin	cheh - to burn
ñ	as in el niño	ñam - to eat *
d	as in doll	dau - to walk
t	as in tender	toat - to be fat
n	as in need	nək - to miss
dt	in between the d and t sound	dtaa - grandfather *
b	as in baby	baay - food, cooked rice
p	as in pretty	pia-saa - language
bp	in between the b and p sound	bpuu - uncle *
m	as in money	mian - to have
y	as in you	yiam - to guard
r	rolled like the Spanish r	rian - to study
l	as in love	luy - money
vw	a combination of the English v and w sound	vwaen-dtaa - glasses *
s	as in sand	siaw-pəu - book
h	as in honey	haal - to dry

Note on Consonants

The /dt/ sound lies between the /d/ and the /t/. Similarly, the /bp/ sound is between the /b/ and /p/. (In linguistic terms, they are both unvoiced and unaspirated.) However, the /vw/ sound is a combination of both sounds, and both are voiced in one double consonant sound. However, when this consonant is used as a final consonant, only the /w/ sound is pronounced. Unlike English, /ng/ can occur at the beginning of words in Cambodian.

Cambodian also has many initial consonant clusters that are not found in English. Some of these sounds are /jr/, /mk/, /pdt/, /dtr/, /tm/, /bd/, /km/, /kn/, and /gd/.

Other final consonant sounds will be represented as follows: /k/ for /g/ and /k/ final consonants; /b/ for /b/, /bp/, and /p/ final consonants; and /t/ for /d/, /dt/, and /t/ final consonants. The letter /y/ will also be used as a final consonant to represent a short /ii/ vowel sound. The /ñ/ final consonant combines an initial /y/ final consonant with a final /n/ final consonant.

Practice the Following Words

A. Words with long vowels:
1. jaan   (ចាន)   - dish, bowl
2. ruub   (រូប)   - picture
3. geeng (គេង)   - to sleep, rest
4. bey   (បី)   - three
5. dtaam (តាម)   - to follow

B. Words with short vowels:
1. gat   (កាត់)   - to cut
2. chob   (ឈប់)   - to stop
3. jet   (ចិត្ត)   - heart
4. dtək   (ទឹក)   - water
5. dtok   (តុ)   - table

C. Words with complex vowels:

1. daɥ (ដើរ) - to walk
2. pliang (ភ្លៀង) - rain
3. jaot (ចោទ) - to accuse
4. rɥang (រឿង) - story
5. gae (កែ) - to correct

D. Words with consonant combination vowels:

1. noam (នាំ) - to lead
2. seh (សេះ) - horse
3. jih (ជិះ) - to ride
4. dtɛang (ទាំង) - including, both
5. dam (ដាំ) - to plant, grow something

E. Words with double consonants:

1. gruu (គ្រូ) - teacher
2. tmeeñ (ធ្មេញ) - tooth
3. pleeng (ភ្លេង) - music
4. bdey (ប្ដី) - husband
5. gbaal (ក្បាល) - head

Similar Consonant and Vowel Sounds

When you are not understood, you are often making subtle errors in pronunciation. Words with similar sounds can have completely different meanings. The length of the vowel is also very important. Try to get the vowel length correct. If you do not, it is easy for others to misunderstand you. Practice saying the following words.

Similar Sound, Different Meaning

1. dtaa (តា) - grandfather
   taa (ថា) - to speak
2. tom (ធំ) - big
   dom (ដុំ) - pile

	dtum	(ទុំ)	- ripe, mature
	tum	(ផុំ)	- to smell
3.	jam	(ចាំ)	- to remember; to wait
	jɔm	(ចំ)	- exactly
4.	dtroo	(ទ្រ)	- to hold, support
	dtrəɥw	(ត្រូវ)	- correct; must
5.	bat	(បាត់)	- to lose, disappear
	bak	(បាក់)	- to break
	baat	(បាត / បាទ)	- bottom; foot; yes particle (male)
6.	bak jəəng	(បាក់ជើង)	- to break your foot
	baat jəəng	(បាតជើង)	- the bottom of your foot
	bɔt jəəng	(បត់ជើង)	- to go to the bathroom
7.	dtaam	(តាម)	- to follow
	dam	(ដាំ)	- to plant, grow
8.	gaat	(កាត)	- card
	kaat	(ខាត)	- to waste, lose
	gat	(កាត់)	- to cut

Short and Long Vowels

1.	jɔɔng	(ចង)	- to tie, bind	jɔng	(ចង់)	- to want
2.	baat	(បាទ)	- yes (male)	bat	(បាត់)	- gone, lost
3.	gaat	(កាត)	- card	gat	(កាត់)	- to cut
4.	dɔɔb	(ដប)	- bottle	dɔb	(ដប់)	- ten

Lesson 1

Greetings; yes-no questions; personal pronouns; numbers, the Cambodian writing system; consonant classes; determining vowel sounds in written Cambodian; consonants and vowels

mee-rian dtii muay   មេរៀន ទី១   Lesson 1

vɛak-a-sab   វាក្យសព្ទ   Vocabulary

kñom	ខ្ញុំ	I, me
nek	អ្នក	you; person[1]
bɔɔng	បង	you (for use with people of your same age group)
look	លោក	you (for use with people who have a high social status)
chmuah	ឈ្មោះ	name
jəm-riab-sua	ជំរាបសួរ	"Hello."
jəm-riab-lia/lia-sen-haꞷy ជំរាបលា / លាសិនហើយ		"Goodbye."
sok-sɔb-baay dtee	សុខសប្បាយទេ	"How are you doing?"[2]
sok-sɔb-baay	សុខសប្បាយ	to be fine
kñom sɔb-baay-jet baan juab look ខ្ញុំសប្បាយចិត្តបានជួបលោក		"Nice to meet you."[3]
ɔt-dtooh	អត់ទោស	"Excuse me."
soom-dtooh	សូមទោស	"I'm sorry."
min-ey-dtee	មិនអីទេ	"It doesn't matter."[4]
ɔɔ-gun/soom ɔɔ-gun	អរគុណ / សូមអរគុណ	"Thank you."
joh	ចុះ	"So, (what about...?)"
vwiñ	វិញ	instead, again
baat	បាទ	yes (male speaker)[5]
jaa	ចាំ	yes (female speaker)[5]
jia / guꞷ-jia	ជា / គឺជា	is, to be
siaw-pəꞷ	សៀវភៅ	book
gaa-saet	កាសែត	newspaper
nia-le-gaa	នាឡិកា	watch, clock
bik	ប៊ិច	pen
kmau-dai	ខ្មៅដៃ	pencil
ga-boob	កាបូប	bag, wallet

nih	នេះ	this
nuh	នោះ	that
a-vwey	អ្វី	what
ey	អី	a common colloquial abbreviation of the word a-vwey (what)
min/ɔt	មិន / អត់	no, not, do not
dtee/ɔt-dtee	ទេ / អត់ទេ	no
dtaʉ	តើ	initial question particle
dtee	ទេ	final question particle[2]
mɛɛn	មែន	right, correct, really
mɛɛn dtee	មែនទេ	"..... right?"
rʉʉ	ឬ	or
gɔɔ	ក៏	also
dae	ដែរ	and, too
yul	យល់	to understand
yul dtee	យល់ទេ	"Understand?"
yul	យល់	"(I) understand."
min yul dtee	មិនយល់ទេ	"(I) don't understand."

Note: 1. *nek* is the generic form of the English word "you." However, it is not used in general speech, and it can actually be considered offensive when used in the wrong situation. For example, if a young person used this word when talking to someone older than them, this would be very socially offensive. Correct forms of the word "you" focus on age, kinship relation, and social status.
2. *sok-sɔb-baay dtee* is more colloquially pronounced *sok-sɔb-baay ey*. The word *dtee* is oftentimes abbreviated in speech to *ey*.
3. The word *look* is used in this phrase for the English word "you." However, other forms of the word "you" can be used according to context.
4. *min-ey-dtee* has the following meanings: "It doesn't matter.", "That's all right.", "Not at all.", "It's nothing.", "Never mind.", "Don't mention it.", "Forget it.", "You're welcome.", and more.
5. *baat* (for male speakers) and *jaa* (for female speakers) are generic forms of the English word "yes." However, "yes" in this sense mainly means an acknowledgment of the other person. It does <u>not</u> always mean an affirmative answer to a question.

vwee-jia-gɔɔ   វេយ្យាករណ៍   **Grammar**

You will be happy to know that Cambodian grammar is very simple. The grammar usually follows a subject-verb-object sentence structure. However, there are no articles (a, an, the) like in English.

e.g. nih jia siaw-pəʉ. = This is a book.
                       (Literally: This is book.)
    nih jia a-vwey? = What is this?
                       (Literally: This is what?)

When telling or asking for a name, do not use the "to be" verb *jia*. Instead, simply use the structure shown below.

e.g. kñom chmuah so-paa. = My name is Sopha.
                       (Literally: I name Sopha.)
    goat chmuah ey? = What is his name?
                       (Literally: He name what?)

dtaʉ (តើ) is the initial particle in a question sentence. It is generally used in formal situations for question sentences that do not form yes-no answers. However, it is optional and is oftentimes not used at all, especially in informal situations.

e.g. (dtaʉ) nih jia a-vwey? = What is this?
                       (Literally: This is what?)

dtee (ទេ) actually has several meanings. First, *dtee* (ទេ) is a question particle that is always placed at the end of question words or phrases that demand a yes or no answer.

e.g. yul dtee? = (Do you) understand?
    look yul, mɛɛn dtee? = You understand, right?

In order to express a negative phrase in Cambodian, the word *min* or *ɔt* is placed before a verb or modifier to indicate that it is a negative phrase. In addition to being a question particle, *dtee* (ទេ) is also used as a final particle in a negative phrase.

e.g. min mɛɛn dtee. = That is not right.
    kñom ɔt yul dtee. = I do not understand.

mɛɛn (មែន) is commonly used in a negative phrase with the verb *jia*. However, it is not used with other verbs.

e.g. nih min mɛɛn jia ga-boob dtee. = This is not a bag.

Conversation 1

Sopha: jəm-riab-sua.

សុផា ជំរាបសួរ

Hello.

John: baat, jəm-riab-sua.

ចន បាទ ជំរាបសួរ

Hello.

Sopha: kñom chmuah so-paa. dtau bɔɔng chmuah ey?

សុផា ខ្ញុំ ឈ្មោះ សុផា តើ បង ឈ្មោះ អី

My name is Sopha. What's your name?

John: kñom chmuah jɔɔn. kñom sɔb-baay-jet baan juab bɔɔng.

ចន ខ្ញុំ ឈ្មោះ ចន ខ្ញុំ សប្បាយចិត្ត បាន ជួប បង

My name is John. Nice to meet you.

Sopha: jaa, kñom gɔɔ sɔb-baay-jet dae.

សុផា ចាំ ខ្ញុំ ក៍ សប្បាយចិត្ត ដែរ

Nice to meet you too.

<u>Conversation 2</u>

Vwan-nak: sok-sɔb-baay dtee?

វណ្ណៈ សុខសប្បាយ ទេ

How are you doing?

Emily: jaa, kñom sok-sɔb-baay. joh bɔɔng viñ, sok-sɔb-baay dtee?

អេមិលី ចាំ ខ្ញុំ សុខសប្បាយ ចុះ បង វិញ សុខសប្បាយ ទេ

I'm fine. How about you?

Vwan-nak: baat kñom sok-sɔb-baay. ɔɔ-gun.

វណ្ណៈ បាទ ខ្ញុំ សុខសប្បាយ អរគុណ

I'm fine. Thank you.

Note: When practicing dialogues such as those above, use the appropriate gender acknowledgement particle (*baat* for males, *jaa* for females).

klia ឃ្លា **Sentences**

1. A: nih jia siaw-pəɯ mɛɛn dtee?
    នេះ ជា សៀវភៅ មែន ទេ
    This a book, right?

    B: baat nih jia siaw-pəɯ.
    បាទ នេះ ជា សៀវភៅ
    Yes, this is a book.

2. A: nih jia nia-le-gaa mɛɛn dtee?
    នេះ ជា នាឡិកា មែន ទេ
    This is a watch, right?

    B: dtee, nih min mɛɛn jia nia-le-gaa dtee.
    ទេ នេះ មិន មែន ជា នាឡិកា ទេ
    No, this is not a watch.

3. A: dtaɯ nih jia a-vwey?
    តើ នេះ ជា អ្វី
    What is this?

    B: nih jia ga-boob.
    នេះ ជា កាបូប
    This is a bag.

4. A: dtaɯ nuh jia kmau-dai rɯɯ bik?
    តើ នោះ ជា ខ្មៅដៃ ឬ ប៊ិច
    Is that a pencil or a pen?

    B: nuh jia bik.
    នោះ ជា ប៊ិច
    That is a pen.

5. A: yul dtee?
    យល់ ទេ
    Do you understand?

    B: yul.
    យល់
    (Yes), I understand.

    C: min yul dtee.
    មិន យល់ ទេ
    No, I don't understand.

6. A: soom-dtooh.
    សូម ទោស
    I'm sorry.
    B: min-ey-dtee.
    មិនអីទេ
    That's all right.

7. A: ɔɔ-gun.
    អរគុណ
    Thank you.
    B: min-ey-dtee.
    មិនអីទេ
    You're welcome.

Note: 1. A lot of Cambodian people greet each other with *yaang meek dae* យ៉ាងម៉េចដែរ ("How is it going?") instead of using *sok-sɔb-baay dtee.*

2. The subject of a sentence is often omitted when understood from the context.
    e.g. A: *kñom sok-sɔb-baay.* = *baat/jaah, sok-sɔb-baay.* ("I'm fine.")

3. Cambodian usually has no direct "yes" or "no." "Yes" or "no" is instead expressed by repeating the main verb or adjective used in the question.
    e.g. A: *yul dtee.* = Understand?
    B: *yul.* = Understand
    C: *min yul dtee.* = Don't understand.
    Be careful not to use *baat* or *jaa* for "yes" all the time. Use this word mainly to acknowledge the other speaker.

4. When saying, "What is this?" the Cambodian phrase "*dtaʉ nih jia a-vwey?*" has the subject and object reversed from its English equivalent. However, Cambodian people often use the more colloquial phrase "*sa-ey nih?* " as well. This puts the object first like in English.

leek លេខ Numbers

0	soon	សូន
1	muay	មួយ
2	bpii	ពីរ
3	bey	បី
4	buan	បួន
5	bpram	ប្រាំ
6	bpram-muay	ប្រាំមួយ
7	bpram-bpii (bpram-bpəl)	ប្រាំពីរ (ប្រាំពីល)[1]
8	bpram-bey	ប្រាំបី
9	bpram-buan	ប្រាំបួន
10	dɔb	ដប់
11	dɔb-muay	ដប់មួយ
12	dɔb-bpii	ដប់ពីរ
16	dɔb-bpram-muay	ដប់ប្រាំមួយ
20	mpei	ម្ភៃ
21	mpei-muay	ម្ភៃមួយ
22	mpei-bpii	ម្ភៃពីរ
26	mpei-bpram-muay	ម្ភៃប្រាំមួយ
30	saam-seb	សាមសិប
31	saam-seb-muay	សាមសិបមួយ
32	saam-seb-bpii	សាមសិបពីរ
36	saam-seb-bpram-muay	សាមសិបប្រាំមួយ
40	sae-seb	សែសិប
50	haa-seb	ហាសិប
60	hok-seb	ហុកសិប
70	jet-seb	ចិតសិប
80	bpaet-seb	ប៉ែតសិប
90	gau-seb	កៅសិប
100	muay rooy	មួយរយ

200	bpii rooy	ពីររយ
600	bpram-muay rooy	ប្រាំមួយរយ
1,000	muay bpoan	មួយពាន់
2,000	bpii bpoan	ពីរពាន់
6,000	bpram-muay bpoan	ប្រាំមួយពាន់
10,000	muay mʉʉn	មួយម៉ឺន
100,000	muay saen	មួយសែន
1,000,000	muay lian	មួយលាន
1,000,000,000	muay bpoan lian	មួយពាន់លាន

Note: 1. Officially this word is pronounced *bpram-bpii*. However, this pronunciation is only used in very formal situations. The word is commonly pronounced *bpram-bpəl*.

2. For ordinal numbers, add dtii (ទី) in front of cardinal numbers.

e.g.   *dtii muay* (ទីមួយ)   = the first
       dtii bpii (ទីពីរ)   = the second
       dtii bey (ទីបី)   = the third
       dtii dɔb (ទីដប់)   = the tenth

Drills

1. Write and say the following sentences in Cambodian using the transliteration system. Also practice saying the sentences.

How are you doing?

_____

My name is _____.

_____

This is a book.

_____

That is not a pen.

_____

2. Use the following words to help form five complete sentences.

chmuah	bik	sok-sɔb-baay
nuh	jia	gaa-saet
bɔɔng	mɛɛn	dtaʉ
dtee	baat	ey
jaa	nih	kñom
min	look	a-vwey

3. Practice saying each word in the vocabulary list in conjunction with the audio recordings. Say the word first, and then wait and listen to the recording. This will help you hear how accurately you are pronouncing the words. It will also help you learn the transliteration system. Then repeat the word again after hearing the correct pronunciation.

Test 1

Match the English words with the Cambodian words.

_____	1.	watch	a.	a-vwey	អ្វី
_____	2.	book	b.	bik	ប៊ិច
_____	3.	pen	c.	nih	នេះ
_____	4.	this	d.	kñom	ខ្ញុំ
_____	5.	I, me	e.	nia-le-gaa	នាឡិកា
_____	6.	also	f.	nuh	នោះ
_____	7.	pencil	g.	gɔɔ	ក៏
_____	8.	name	h.	chmuah	ឈ្មោះ
_____	9.	what	i.	ga-boob	កាប៊ូប
_____	10.	bag	j.	siaw-pəu	សៀវភៅ
			k.	kmau-dai	ខ្មៅដៃ

Translate the following sentences into English or Cambodian.

1. dtau bɔɔng chmuah ey?
តើ បង ឈ្មោះ អ្វី

_____

2. baat, kñom sok-sɔb-baay.
បាទ ខ្ញុំ សុខសប្បាយ

_____

3. dtau nih jia siaw-pəu ruu ga-boob?
តើ នេះ ជា សៀវភៅ ឬ កាប៊ូប

_____

4. How are you doing?

_____

5. This is a newpaper, right?

_____

The Cambodian Writing System

The Cambodian writing system may look difficult at first, but you will soon find that it is much easier than it appears. Cambodian is a phonetic alphabet that, unlike English, has very few exceptions to it rules. The alphabet has thirty-three basic consonant symbols and thirty-two lower-case sub-consonant symbols. There are also twenty-four vowel symbols. In addition, there are eleven independent vowel symbols. Altogether that makes 100 different symbols in the Cambodian alphabet, and that does not include punctuation markers. However, don't let this discourage you. Cambodian script is very easy to learn, and you will soon be reading and writing Cambodian yourself. We promise!

In just a few pages, you will begin your study of the Cambodian script. By learning the script from the beginning, you will reap many benefits. Your pronunciation and comprehension will improve. If you are traveling to Cambodia, you will be able to immediately recognize many street signs and symbols. Learning the script will also solidify a base of knowledge for future study.

The transliteration system in this book strives to provide the best possible representation of the sounds in the Cambodian language. However, this is not easily accomplished. We encourage you to use the transliteration system in your early days of study, but it is wise to stop using it as soon as possible. This will help you learn the script more quickly by not forcing you to rely on the transliteration. Eventually you will be able to read Cambodian so well, you will not have to rely on the transliteration at all, and you may even have trouble reading it!

<u>Consonant Classes</u>

There are two classes of consonants: /ɔɔ/ consonants (a-koo-sa) and /oo/ consonants (koo-sa). There are fifteen /ɔɔ/ consonants and eighteen /oo/ consonants. The only difference between the two classes of consonants is fairly obvious. The /ɔɔ/ consonants emit a natural /ɔɔ/ vowel sound and the /oo/ consonants emit a natural /oo/ vowel sound. When combined with a vowel, the class of the consonant affects what vowel sound is rendered. This book will introduce you to both consonant classes at once. In just a short time, you will be able to start making sense of all the squiggly lines you have been seeing so far!

Consonants ព្យញ្ជនៈ pjuañ-jia-nɛa

These are the first ten consonants in the Cambodian alphabet. They are a mixture the of /ɔɔ/ and /oo/ consonants. The consonant class can be determined by the natural vowel sound.

Consonant	Pronunciation	Sound
ក	gɔɔ	/g/
ខ	kɔɔ	/k/
គ	goo	/g/
ឃ	koo	/k/
ង	ngoo	/ng/
ច	jɔɔ	/j/
ឆ	chɔɔ	/ch/
ជ	joo	/j/
ឈ	choo	/ch/
ញ	ñoo	/ñ/

Practice Writing Consonants

Practice writing the following consonants. Remember to use the proper stroke order as shown below.

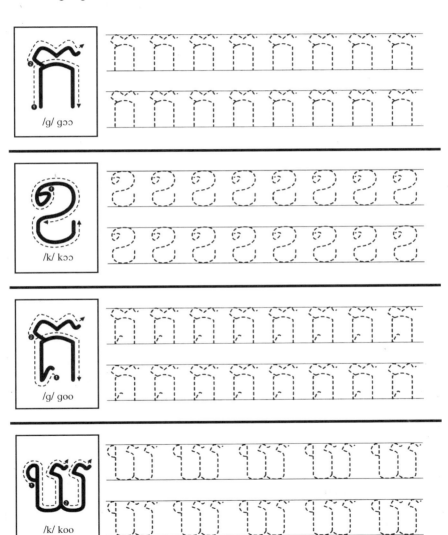

/ng/ ngoo

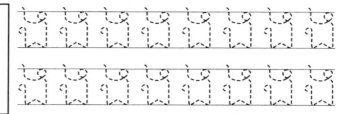

/j/ jɔɔ

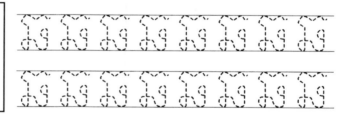

/ch/ chɔɔ

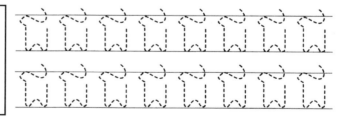

/j/ joo

/ch/ choo

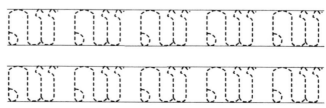

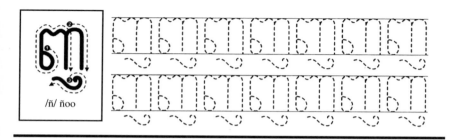

/ñ/ ñoo

Vowels ស្រៈ sra

Cambodian has twenty-four basic vowel symbols which can have different sounds depending on the consonant used. Most of these vowels have two sounds, one for /ɔɔ/ consonants and one for /oo/ consonants. However, many vowels have only one sound for both consonant classes. Vowels can either have long or short sounds.

All standard vowels must be combined with a consonant. Consonant sounds always precede the vowel sound. However, the vowel can be placed in front of, on top of, below, or around the consonant. In fact, many beginning students may think they are reading in circles! In the vowels below, the consonant is represented by a dash. The sounds for /ɔɔ/ and /oo/ series consonants are both shown.

Cambodian also has eleven independent vowels that are used without an accompanying consonant. These vowels are not used very often, and they will be introduced later.

Vowel	Vowel Name	Sound /ɔɔ/-/oo/
$-$ា	sra aa	/aa/-/ia/
$-$ិ	sra e	/e/-/i/
$-$ី	sra ey	/ey/-/ii/

	sra ə	/ə/
	sra ɯɯ	/ɯɯ/
	sra o	/o/-/u/
	sra oo	/oo/-/uu/

Consonant Vowel Combinations

Here are some examples of consonant-vowel combinations to show you how consonant-vowel sounds are produced.

គ (gɔɔ) + ា (aa) = គា (gaa) -- (/ɔɔ/ series consonant produces the /aa/ sound)

ក (goo) + ា (ia) = កា (gia) -- (/oo/ series consonant produces the /ia/ sound)

ឈ (choo) + ឺ (ɯɯ) = ឈឺ (chɯɯ)

ជ (jɔɔ) + ុ (oo) = ជុ (joo)

ញ (ñoo) + ី (ii) = ញី (ñii)

ខ (kɔɔ) + ា (aa) + ង (ngoo) = ខាង (kaang)

Note: Final consonants do not emit their natural /ɔɔ/ or /oo/ vowel sound.

Practice Writing the Following Vowels

Use ñ as the consonant when practicing the following vowels.

កា កា កា កា កា

កឺ កឺ កឺ កឺ កឺ

កឹ កឹ កឹ កឹ កឹ

កឺ កឺ កឺ កឺ កឺ

កឺ កឺ កឺ កឺ កឺ

កោ កោ កោ កោ កោ

កៅ កៅ កៅ កៅ កៅ

Read the Following Aloud

1. កា កិ កី កឹ កឺ កុ កូ

2. ខា ខិ ខី ខឹ ខឺ ខុ ខូ

3. គា គិ គី គឹ គឺ គុ គូ

4. យា យិ យី យឹ យឺ យុ យូ

5. ងា ងិ ងី ងឹ ងឺ ងុ ងូ

6. ចា ចិ ចី ចឹ ចឺ ចុ ចូ

7. អា អិ អី អឹ អឺ អុ អូ

8. ជា ជិ ជី ជឹ ជឺ ជុ ជូ

9. ឈា ឈិ ឈី ឈឹ ឈឺ ឈុ ឈូ

10. ញា ញិ ញី ញឹ ញឺ ញុ ញូ

Writing Exercise 1

Transcribe the following sounds into Cambodian script. There may be several ways to spell some of the sounds.

1. kaa _____

2. gee _____

3. nguu _____

4. je _____

5. guu _____

6. ngu _____

7. gaa _____

8. jia _____

9. kii _____

10. ñii _____

11. chʉʉ _____

12. jey _____

13. ñia _____

14. go _____

15. kia _____

16. ñʉʉ _____

17. ko _____

18. chey _____

19. ngia _____

20. ju _____

Lesson 2

nəʉ (at); *mian* (to have); more pronouns;
more consonants and vowels

mee-rian dtii bpii មេរៀន ទី២ Lesson 2

vɛak-a-sab វាក្យសព្ទ Vocabulary

dtuu-re-sab	ទូរស័ព្ទ	telephone
vwaen-dtaa	វ៉ែនតា	eye-glasses
luy	លុយ	money
ruub/ruub-tɔɔt	រូប / រូបថត	picture; photograph
maa-sin-tɔɔt-ruub	ម៉ាស៊ីនថតរូប	camera
vwɛah-ja-naa-nu-grɔɔm	វចនានុក្រម	dictionary
grɔ-dah	ក្រដាស	paper
dtok	តុ	table
grɛɛ	គ្រែ	bed
gau-ey	កៅអី	chair
tvwia	ទ្វារ	door, opening
bɔɔng-uik	បង្អួច	window
bɔn-dtub	បន្ទប់	room
bɔn-dtub-geeng	បន្ទប់គេង	bedroom
bɔn-dtub-dtək	បន្ទប់ទឹក	bathroom
pdtɛah	ផ្ទះ	house, home
nəɰ/nəɰ-ae	នៅ / នៅង	at, to be somewhere (live, stay)
nəɰ nih	នៅនេះ	over here
nəɰ nuh	នៅនោះ	over there
nəɰ nɔh	នៅណោះ	over there (farther)
naa	ណា	which; where
nəɰ naa/nəɰ ae naa	នៅណា / នៅងណា	where
knong	ក្នុង	in
ləə	លើ	on, above
graom	ក្រោម	under

gɔn-daal កណ្ដាល	between
kaang ខាង	way, direction
chvweeng ឆ្វេង	left
sdam ស្ដាំ	right
haʉy/haʉy-nəng ហើយ / ហើយនិង	and[1]
mian មាន	to have
mook មក	to come
bpii ពី	from
mook bpii មកពី	come from
bprɔ-dteeh/srok ប្រទេស/ស្រុក	country[2]
bprɔ-dteeh kmae/srok kmae/gam-bpu-jia ប្រទេសខ្មែរ / ស្រុកខ្មែរ / កម្ពុជា	Cambodia[3]
bprɔ-dteeh/srok jen ប្រទេស/ស្រុក ចិន	China
bprɔ-dteeh/srok jo-bpun ប្រទេស/ស្រុក ជប៉ុន	Japan
bprɔ-dteeh/srok tai ប្រទេស/ស្រុក ថៃ	Thailand
bprɔ-dteeh/srok vwiat-naam ប្រទេស/ស្រុក វៀតណាម	Vietnam
bprɔ-dteeh/srok aa-mee-rik ប្រទេស/ស្រុក អាមេរិក	America
roat រដ្ឋ	state
rian រៀន	to learn, study
pia-saa ភាសា	language
pia-saa kmae ភាសាខ្មែរ	Cambodian language
pia-saa ɔng-glee ភាសាអង់គ្លេស	English language
pia-saa baa-rang ភាសាបារាំង	French language
bpi-baak ពិបាក	difficult
srual ស្រួល	easy
nah ណាស់	very[4]
yəəng/yəəng kñom យើង / យើងខ្ញុំ	we, us[5]
goat គាត់	he, she, him, her[6]
gee/bpuak gee គេ / ពួកគេ	they, them
vwia វា	it

1. *hauy* is generally used for the word "and" when setting off a seperate clause. *hauy-nəng* or simply *nəng* can be used as "and" when listing seperate items.
2. *bprɔ-dteeh* is more formal than *srok,* but both are acceptable.
3. The word *gam-bpu-jia* (កម្ពុជា) is the formal name for Cambodia. It is not necessary to use *srok* or *bprɔ-dteeh* in front of this word.
4. *nah* is a common emphasizer that can mean either "very," "very much," etc.
5. *yəəng* means "all of us." *yəəng kñom* means a group of people on the speaker's side of the conversation.
6. *goat* is usually used when talking about people who are either older or have a higher social status than the speaker. *gee* can be used when talking about people who have the same or lower age and social status as the speaker. However, *goat* is a more polite term even under these circumstances. There are no gender distinctions in either of these words.

vwee-jia-gɔɔ វេយ្យាករណ៍ **Grammar**

The words *nəu* and *nəu-ae* have several similar meanings. The first meaning is equivalent to the word "at" or "to be at."
e.g. kñom nəu pdtɛah. = I'm at home.
(Literally: I at home.)
Another meaning is "to live at."
e.g. kñom nəu ook-lun. = I live in Oakland.
(Literally: I live at Oakland.)
ae also means "at." It can be used with *nəu.*
e.g. dtau goat nəu-ae naa? = Where is he?
(Literally: He at where?)

naa acts as a modifier to form the equivalent of the words "which" and "where." It is important to again note that modifiers generally come after the words they modify.
e.g. ruub muay naa? = Which picture?
(Literally: Picture one which?)
goat nəu naa? = Where is he?
(Literally: He at where?)
dtau bɔɔng mook bpii naa? = Where are you from?
(Literally: You from where?)

mian means "to have" and is used as shown below.
e.g. kñom mian dtuu-re-sab. = I have a telephone.
(Literally: I have telephone.)

dae can be used at the end of phrases that start with the word *joh* to form "And, so..." type questions.
e.g. joh bɔɔng chmuah ey dae? = And, so what's your name?
(Literally: So you name what also?)

In Cambodian, modifiers are placed after the word they modify. Unlike English, there is never a "to be" verb placed between a word and a modifier. The "to be" verb *jia* is only placed between a subject and an object.
e.g. pia-saa kmae srual. = Cambodian is easy.
Verbs can also modify a modifier.
e.g. pia-saa kmae srual rian. = Cambodian is easy to learn.

<u>Conversation 1</u>

Sopheap: dtau look mook bpii naa?

សុភាព តើ លោក មក ពី ណា

Where are you from?

Tom: kñom mook bpii srok aa-mee-rik. joh nek mook bpii naa dae?

ថម ខ្ញុំ មក ពី ស្រុក អាមេរិក ចុះ អ្នក មក ពី ណា ដែរ

I am from America. So, where are you from?

Sopheap: kñom mook bpii srok kmae. kñom nau pnom bpeeñ. dtau look nau ae naa dae?

សុភាព ខ្ញុំ មក ពី ស្រុក ខ្មែរ ខ្ញុំ នៅ ភ្នំ ពេញ តើ លោក នៅ ឯ ណា ដែរ

I am from Cambodia. I live in Phnom Penh. Where do you live?

Tom: kñom nau roat kaa-lii-hvwoo-ñaa.

ថម ខ្ញុំ នៅ រដ្ឋ ខាលីហ្វោញ៉ា

I live in California.

__Conversation 2__

Srey: dtau look rian kaang ey?[1,2]
ស្រី   តើ លោក រៀន ខាង អី
        What are you studying?

Rick: kñom rian kaang pia-saa kmae.
រិក   ខ្ញុំ រៀន ខាង ភាសា ខ្មែរ
        I am studying Cambodian.

Srey: pia-saa kmae bpi-baak rian dtee?
ស្រី   ភាសា ខ្មែរ ពិបាក រៀន ទេ
        Is Cambodian difficult to learn?

Rick: min bpi-baak dtee. pia-saa kmae srual nah. joh bɔɔng
        rian pia-saa ey dae?
រិក   មិន ពិបាក ទេ ភាសា ខ្មែរ ស្រួល ណាស់ ចុះ បង
        រៀន ភាសា អី ដែរ
        It's not difficult. Cambodian is very easy. So, what
        language are you studying?

Srey: kñom rian pia-saa jen. pia-saa jen min srual rian dtee.
ស្រី   ខ្ញុំ រៀន ភាសា ចិន ភាសា ចិន មិន ស្រួល រៀន ទេ
        I am studying Chinese. Chinese is not easy to learn.

Note: 1. *kaang* is normally used to show direction (*kaang nih* = this way),
           but kaang can also mean a direction of study (i.e. what you are
           studying).
        2. Be sure to remember that *ey* is a colloquial abbreviation of *a-vwey*.
           It is used frequently.

klia ឃ្លា **Sentences**

1.   A: bik nəʉ naa?
ប៊ិច នៅ ណា
Where is the pen?
  B: bik nəʉ nih.
ប៊ិច នៅ នេះ
The pen is right here.

2.   A: ruub-tɔɔt nəʉ naa?
រូបថត នៅ ណា
Where is the photograph?
  B: ruub-tɔɔt nəʉ graom gau-ey.
រូបថត នៅ ក្រោម កៅអី
The photograph is below the chair.

3.   A: bɔɔng kim nəʉ naa?
បង ឃីម នៅ ណា
Where is Kim?
  B: bɔɔng kim nəʉ srok baa-rang.
បង ឃីម នៅ ស្រុកបារាំង
Kim is in France.

4.   A: vwaen-dtaa nəʉ ae naa?
វ៉ែនតា នៅ ឯ ណា
Where are the glasses?
  B: vwaen-dtaa nəʉ ləə grɛɛ.
វ៉ែនតា នៅ លើ គ្រែ
The glasses are on top of the bed.

5.   A: gau-ey nəʉ naa?
កៅអី នៅ ណា
Where is the chair?
  B: gau-ey nəʉ knong bɔn-dtub-geeng.
កៅអី នៅ ក្នុង បន្ទប់គេង
The chair is in the bedroom.

6.   A: bprɔ-dteeh kmae nəʉ ae naa?
ប្រទេស ខ្មែរ នៅ ឯ ណា
Where is Cambodia?

B: bprɔ-dteeh kmae nəʉ gɔn-daal bprɔ-dteeh tai nəng
bprɔ-dteeh vwiat-naam.
ប្រទេស ខ្មែរ នៅ កណ្ដាល ប្រទេស ថៃ និង ប្រទេស វៀតណាម
Cambodia is in-between Thailand and Vietnam.

7. A: bɔn-dtub-dtək nəʉ kaang naa?
បន្ទប់ទឹក នៅ ខាង ណា
Which way is the restroom?

B: bɔn-dtub-dtək nəʉ kaang chvweeng.
បន្ទប់ទឹក នៅ ខាង ឆ្វេង
The bathroom is on the left.

C: bɔn-dtub-dtək nəʉ kaang sdam.
បន្ទប់ទឹក នៅ ខាង ស្ដាំ
The bathroom is on the right.

8. A: dtaʉ goat mian a-vwey?
តើ គាត់ មាន អ្វី
What does she have?

B: goat mian maa-sin-tɔɔt-ruub.
គាត់ មាន ម៉ាស៊ីនថតរូប
She has a camera.

9. A: pdtɛah goat mian bɔn-dtub-dtək dtee?
ផ្ទះ គាត់ មាន បន្ទប់ទឹក ទេ
Does his house have a bathroom?

B: jaa, pdtɛah goat mian bɔn-dtub-dtək.
ថា ផ្ទះ គាត់ មាន បន្ទប់ទឹក
Yes, his house has a bathroom.

C: pdtɛah goat ɔt mian bɔn-dtub-dtək dtee.
ផ្ទះ គាត់ អត់ មាន បន្ទប់ទឹក ទេ
His house does not have a bathroom.

10. A: bɔn-dtub-geeng goat mian a-vwey?
បន្ទប់គេង គាត់ មាន អ្វី
What does she have in her bedroom?

B: bɔn-dtub-geeng goat mian gau-ey dtok nəng grɛɛ.
បន្ទប់គេង គាត់ មាន កៅអី តុ និង គ្រែ
Her bedroom has a chair, table, and bed.

11. A: dtau goat rian pia-saa ɔng-glee dtee?
    តើ គាត់ រៀន ភាសា អង់គ្លេស ទេ
    Is she learning English?

   B: baat, goat rian pia-saa ɔng-glee.
    បាទ គាត់ រៀន ភាសា អង់គ្លេស
    Yes, she is learning English.

   C: goat min rian pia-saa ɔng-glee dtee.
    គាត់ មិន រៀន ភាសា អង់គ្លេស ទេ
    She is not learning English.

12. A: dtau goat rian pia-saa kmae bpii naa?
    តើ គាត់ រៀន ភាសា ខ្មែរ ពី ណា
    Where did he learn Cambodian?

   B: goat rian pia-saa kmae bpii vwɛah-ja-naa-nu-grɔɔm.
    គាត់ រៀន ភាសា ខ្មែរ ពី វចនានុក្រម
    He learned Cambodian from a dictionary.

13. A: dtau so-paa rian pia-saa a-vwey?
    តើ សុផា រៀន ភាសា អ្វី
    What language does Sopha study?

   B: so-paa rian pia-saa baa-rang.
    សុផា រៀន ភាសា បារាំង
    Sopha studies French.

Note: Some English translations of these sentences assume a certain tense. Most are in the present tense. However, these same sentences can be correctly translated into other tenses as well. This is because tenses in spoken Cambodian are often determined through context.

Drills

1. Write and say the following sentences in Cambodian.

   The paper is on top of the table.

   _____

   Susan is in Cambodia.

   _____

   I am studying Cambodian.

   _____

   Sopha is from Phnom Penh.

   _____

2. Using the transliteration system, write a paragraph with sentences explaining the following:
   Where you are from.
   Where you live.
   What language you are studying.
   Whether the language is easy or difficult.

3. Use the following words to help form ten sentences.

nəʉ	kñom	pdtɛah
srual	rian	dtuu-re-sab
bɔɔng	mian	pia-saa ɔng-glee
a-vwey	kaang	gau-ey
ləə	luy	srok aa-mee-rik
goat	grɛɛ	pia-saa kmae
knong	graom	gɔn-daal
chvweeng	ɔt	bɔn-dtub-dtək
dtee	sdam	bɔn-dtub-geeng

Test 2

Match the English words with the Cambodian words.

_____ 1. America   a. chvweeng   ឆ្វេង
_____ 2. table   b. graom   ក្រោម
_____ 3. money   c. gam-bpu-jia   កម្ពុជា
_____ 4. left   d. nəʉ   នៅ
_____ 5. Cambodia   e. bɔn-dtub-geeng   បន្ទប់គេង
_____ 6. language   f. knong   ក្នុង
_____ 7. in   g. srok-aa-mee-rik   ស្រុកអាមេរិក
_____ 8. house   h. bpii   ពី
_____ 9. under   i. luy   លុយ
_____ 10. telephone   j. srual   ស្រួល
_____ 11. bedroom   k. dtok   តុ
_____ 12. from   l. pdtɛah   ផ្ទះ
_____ 13. he/she   m. gɔn-daal   កណ្ដាល
_____ 14. easy   n. sdtam   ស្ដាំ
_____ 15. between   o. pia-saa   ភាសា
                              p. bɔn-dtub-dtək   បន្ទប់ទឹក
                              q. dtuu-re-sab   ទូរស័ព្ទ
                              r. goat   គាត់

Translate the following into English or Cambodian.

1. luy nəʉ knong ga-boob.

    លុយ នៅ ក្នុង កាប៉ូប

    _____

2. kñom mian grɛɛ nəng dtok.

    ខ្ញុំ មាន គ្រែ និង តុ

    _____

3. dtaʉ goat mook bpii bprɔ-dteeh aa-mee-rik rʉʉ bprɔ-dteeh
    baa-rang?

    តើ គាត់ មក ពី ប្រទេស អាមេរិក ឬ ប្រទេស
    បារាំង

    _____

4. The telephone is on top of the table.

    _____

5. I am studying Cambodian and Chinese.

    _____

Consonants ព្យញ្ជនៈ pjuañ-jia-nɛa

These are seven more consonants in the Cambodian alphabet. These consonants are also a mixture the of /ɔɔ/ and /oo/ consonant classes.

Consonant	Pronunciation	Sound
ឌ	dɔɔ	/d/
ណ	nɔɔ	/n/
ត	dtɔɔ	/dt/
ថ	tɔɔ	/t/
ទ	dtoo	/dt/
ធ	too	/t/
ន	noo	/n/

Practice Writing Consonants

Practice writing the following consonants. Remember to use the proper stroke order as shown below.

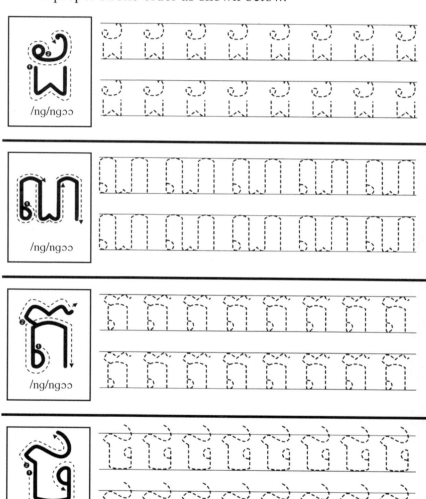

/dt/ dtoo

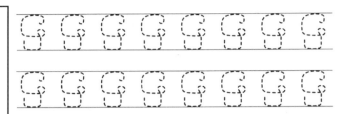

/t/ too

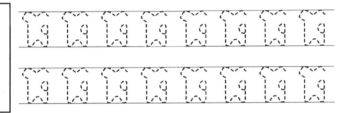

/n/ noo

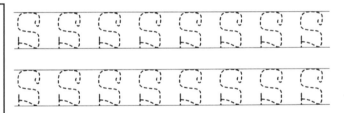

More Vowels ស្រៈ sra

The following vowels are the next seven vowels in the Cambodian alphabet. Remember to distinguish between the /ɔɔ/ and /oo/ consonant classes when forming vowel sounds. However, most of these vowels have only one sound for both classes of consonants.

Vowel	Vowel Name	Sound /ɔɔ/-/oo/
ឹ	sra ua	/ua/
ើ	sra au	/au/-/əə/
ឿ	sra ʉa	/ʉa/
ៀ	sra ia	/ia/
េ	sra ee	/ee/
ែ	sra ae	/ae/-/ɛɛ/
ៃ	sra ai	/ai/-/ei/

Practice Writing the Following Vowels

Use ញ /-/ as the consonant when practicing the following vowels.

ក្ឈ ក្ឈ ក្ឈ ក្ឈ

 កើ កើ កើ កើ

កឿ កឿ កឿ កឿ

កៀ កៀ កៀ កៀ

កេ កេ កេ កេ

កែ កែ កែ កែ

កៃ កៃ កៃ កៃ

Read The Following Aloud

1. ដួ ដើ ដៀ្យី ដៀ្យ ដេ ដែ ដៃ

2. ណួ ណើ ណៀ្យី ណៀ្យ ណេ ណែ ណៃ

3. តួ តើ តៀ្យី តៀ្យ តេ តែ តៃ

4. ថួ ថើ ថៀ្យី ថៀ្យ ថេ ថែ ថៃ

5. ទួ ទើ ទៀ្យី ទៀ្យ ទេ ទែ ទៃ

6. ធួ ធើ ធៀ្យី ធៀ្យ ធេ ធែ ធៃ

7. នួ នើ នៀ្យី នៀ្យ នេ នែ នៃ

Reading Exercise: Read the following words and practice writing them in Cambodian.

1. ឈើ wood 2. កែ to correct

3. គូ partner 4. តុ table

5. ខែ month 6. ថែ to care for

7. គួ body, shape 8. ជឿ to believe

9. ណា which, where 10. តើ question particle

11. គេ them 12. ដៃ hand, arm

13. ថៃ Thai 14. ទូ cabinet

Writing Exercise 2

Transcribe the following sounds into Cambodian script. There may be several ways to spell some of the sounds.

1. dtia _____

2. taa _____

3. tia _____

4. chei _____

5. nɔɔ _____

6. ñɯa _____

7. ti _____

8. dtaa _____

9. jai _____

10. jua _____

11. ngɯa _____

12. nae _____

13. dee _____

14. nəə _____

15. gua _____

16. ney _____

17. təə _____

18. ñia _____

19. dtei _____

20. dtə _____

Lesson 3

jɔng (to want), *dtəʉ* (to go); verb combinations;
asking for permission; more vowels and consonants

mee-rian dtii bey មេរៀន ទី៣ Lesson 3

vɛak-a-sab វាក្យសព្ទ Vocabulary

psaa	ផ្សារ	market
yun-hɔh	យន្តហោះ	airplane
vwial-yun-hɔh	វាលយន្តហោះ	airport
saa-laa/saa-laa-rian	សាលា / សាលារៀន	school
mo-haa-vwi-dtyia-lay	មហាវិទ្យាល័យ	college
sa-gɔɔl-vwi-dtyia-lay	សាកលវិទ្យាល័យ	university
tnak/tnak-rian	ថ្នាក់/ថ្នាក់រៀន	class
ban-naa-lay	បណ្ណាល័យ	library
poo-ja-nii-taan	ភោជនីយដ្ឋាន	restaurant
haang/psaa	ហាង / ផ្សារ	store
haang-jak-sang	ហាងចាក់សាំង	gas station
haang-lok-siaw-pəɯ	ហាងលក់សៀវភៅ	book store
staa-nii	ស្ថានីយ	station
ro-dteh-pləəng	រទេះភ្លើង	train
staa-nii ro-dteh-pləəng	ស្ថានីយរទេះភ្លើង	train station
mon-dtii-bpeet	មន្ទីរពេទ្យ	hospital
bprai-sa-nii/bpoh	ប្រៃសណីយ/ប៉ុស	post office
to-nia-gia/bɔng	ធនាគារ/បង់	bank
staan-dtuut	ស្ថានទូត	embassy
soom	សូម	please
dtəɯ	ទៅ	to go
ni-yiay	និយាយ	to speak
sdab	ស្ដាប់	to listen; understand
jɔng	ចង់	to want
dtiñ	ទិញ	to buy
ñam	ញ៉ាំ	to eat, ingest[1]
baay	បាយ	food; cooked rice[2]

tvwəə ធ្វើ	to do; to make
tvwəə-gaa ធ្វើការ	to work
jool-jet ចូលចិត្ត	to like, prefer
məəl មើល	to watch
gon កុន	movie
roong-gon រោងកុន	movie theater
dtuu-rə-dtuah ទូរទស្សន៍	television
geeng/deek គេង / ដេក	to sleep
leeng លេង	to play
gey-laa/bal កីឡា / បាល់	sports, athletics[3]
bal-dtoat បាល់ទាត់	soccer
bal-dtɛah បាល់ទះ	volleyball
pleeng ភ្លេង	music
aaik អាច	can
baan បាន	possible; to get
klah ខ្លះ	some
jeh ចេះ	to know how to do something
bɔn-dtek-bɔn-dtuuik បន្តិចបន្តួច	a little bit
aan អាន	to read
sɔɔ-see សរសេរ	to write
ak-sɔɔ អក្សរ	alphabet, script
ak-sɔɔ kmae អក្សរខ្មែរ	Cambodian alphabet
ak-sɔɔ ɔng-glee/ɔk-sɔɔ baa-rang អក្សរអង់គ្លេស / អក្សរបារាំង	Roman alphabet
ak-sɔɔ tai អក្សរថៃ	Thai alphabet
ak-sɔɔ jen អក្សរចិន	Chinese characters

1. *ñam* commonly means "to eat." However, the word can also mean "to drink." The literal meaning is "to ingest." Cambodian has several other words with this same meaning that are used according to context. *ñam* is also very rarely used alone. It is commonly used before the word *baay*.
2. In Cambodian, *baay* can mean either food or cooked rice. This double meaning is most likely due to the fact that Cambodians eat rice with almost every meal. Due to the abundance of rice in Cambodian society, Cambodian has other words for different forms of rice.
3. *bal* is a commonly used term for sports that use a ball.

vwee-jia-gɔɔ វេយ្យាករណ៍ **Grammar**

You will now be introduced to verb combinations in the Cambodian language. This is the equivalent to a verb plus a infinitive phrase. Cambodian combines verbs to form such phrases.
e.g. kñom jɔng dtəu psaa. = I want to go to the market.
(Literally: I want go market.)
goat jɔng dtəu ñam baay. = He wants to go eat.
(Literally: He want go eat food.)

baan is a very important word in the Cambodian language and has several meanings. *baan* roughly means "can," "possible," or "able." It is always used at the end of a sentence.
e.g. kñom dtəu baan. = I can go. (Literally: I go possible.)

When asking permission in Cambodian, *baan* is placed at the end of the sentence followed by the final question particle *dtee*.
e.g. kñom soom dtəu psaa, baan dtee? =
May I please go to the market?
Answers to permission questions also include *baan*.
dtəu baan = (You) may go.

baan can also be used with the negative particle *dtee* to form negative phrases, including negative answers to permission questions.
e.g. nek dtəu min baan dtee. = You cannot go.
kñom tvwəə min baan dtee. = I cannot do it.

aaik also means "can" and is often inserted before the verb in sentences where *baan* is used.
e.g. kñom aaik tvwəə baan. = I can do it.
(Literally: I can do possible.)

jeh means to know how to do something.
e.g. kñom jeh aan. = I can read. / I know how to read.

klah literally means "some" and is often used at the end of question sentences. Even though this particle is optional, a sentence can sometimes sound awkward if it is not used.
e.g. bɔng jɔng tvwəə ey klah? = What do you want to do?
(Literally: You want do what some?)
A more literal translation would be "What are some of the things you want to do."

<u>Conversation 1</u>

Sopia: dtaʉ bɔɔng jɔng dtəʉ naa?
សុភា   តើ   បង   ចង់   ទៅ   ណា
Where do you want to go?

John: kñom jɔng dtəʉ məəl gon.
ចន   ខ្ញុំ   ចង់   ទៅ   មើល   កុន
I want to go watch a movie.

Sopia: kñom min jɔng dtəʉ məəl gon dtee.
សុភា   ខ្ញុំ   មិន   ចង់   ទៅ   មើល   កុន   ទេ
I don't want to go watch a movie.

John: dtaʉ bɔɔng jɔng dtəʉ naa vwiñ
ចន   តើ   បង   ចង់   ទៅ   ណា   វិញ
Where would you like to go instead?

Sopia: kñom jɔng dtəʉ məəl gey-laa. dtəʉ baan dtee?
សុភា   ខ្ញុំ   ចង់   ទៅ   មើល   កីឡា   ទៅ   បាន   ទេ
I want to go watch a sporting event? Can we go?

John: baan.
ចន   បាន
That's fine.

Conversation 2

Sovann:	dtaɯ nek jeh ni-yiay pia-saa kmae dtee?
សុវណ្ណ	តើ អ្នក ចេះ និយាយ ភាសា ខ្មែរ ទេ
	Can you speak Cambodian?
Jill:	jaa, kñom jeh ni-yiay pia-saa kmae.
ជិល	ចា៎ ខ្ញុំ ចេះ និយាយ ភាសា ខ្មែរ
	Yes, I can speak Cambodian.
Sovann:	dtaɯ nek jeh sɔɔ-see ak-sɔɔ kmae dtee?
សុវណ្ណ	តើ អ្នក ចេះ សរសេរ អក្សរ ខ្មែរ ទេ
	Can you write the Cambodian alphabet?
Jill:	jaa, kñom jeh sɔɔ-see bɔn-dtek-bɔn-dtuuik.
ជិល	ចា៎ ខ្ញុំ ចេះ សរសេរ បន្តិចបន្តួច
	Yes, I can write a little bit.

klia   ឃ្លា   **Sentences**

1.   A: bɔɔng dtəɰ naa?
         បង   ទៅ   ណា
         Where are you going?

      B: kñom dtəɰ to-nia-gia.
         ខ្ញុំ   ទៅ   ធនាគារ
         I am going to the bank.

      C: kñom dtəɰ vial-yun-hɔh.
         ខ្ញុំ   ទៅ   វាលយន្តហោះ
         I am going to the airport.

2.   A: dtaɰ nek jɔng dtiñ a-vwey?
         តើ   អ្នក ចង់ ទិញ   អ្វី
         What would you like to buy?

      B: kñom jɔng dtiñ dtuu-rə-dtuah.
         ខ្ញុំ   ចង់   ទិញ   ទូរទស្សន៍
         I want to buy a television.

3.   A: dtaɰ goat jool-jet tvwəə ey klah?
         តើ   គាត់ ចូលចិត្ត ធ្វើ   អី ខ្លះ
         What does she like to do.

      B: goat jool-jet leeng pleeng.
         គាត់   ចូលចិត្ត លេង   ភ្លេង
         She likes to play music.

4.   A: bɔɔng jɔng dtəɰ ban-naa-lay dtee?
         បង   ចង់ ទៅ   បណ្ណាល័យ   ទេ
         Do you want to go to the library?

      B: baat, kñom jɔng dtəɰ.
         បាទ   ខ្ញុំ   ចង់ ទៅ
         Yes, I want to go.

C: kñom min jɔng dtəʉ ban-naa-lay dtee.

ខ្ញុំ មិន ចង់ ទៅ បណ្ណាល័យ ទេ

I don't want to go to the library.

5. A: dtaʉ bɔɔng jɔng dtəʉ ñam baay nəʉ ae naa?

តើ បង ចង់ ទៅ ញ៉ាំ បាយ នៅ ឯ ណា

Where would you like to go eat?

B: kñom jɔng dtəʉ ñam baay nəʉ poo-ja-nii-taan.

ខ្ញុំ ចង់ ទៅ ញ៉ាំ បាយ នៅ ភោជនីយដ្ឋាន

I want to go eat at a restaurant.

C: kñom jɔng dtəʉ ñam baay nəʉ pdtɛah.

ខ្ញុំ ចង់ ទៅ ញ៉ាំ បាយ នៅ ផ្ទះ

I want to go eat at home.

6. A: kñom soom dtəʉ bɔn-dtub-dtək baan dtee?

ខ្ញុំ សូម ទៅ បន្ទប់ទឹក បាន ទេ

May I please go to the bathroom?

B: baan.

បាន

Yes, you may.[1]

C: min baan dtee/dtəʉ min baan dtee.

មិន បាន ទេ / ទៅ មិន បាន ទេ

No, you may not.

7. A: kñom soom dtəʉ leeng bal-dtɛah baan dtee?

ខ្ញុំ សូម ទៅ លេង បាល់ទះ បាន ទេ

May I please go play volleyball?

B: baan.

បាន

Yes, you may.

C: min baan dtee/dtəʉ min baan dtee.

មិន បាន ទេ / ទៅ មិន បាន ទេ

No, you may not.

8.   A: dtaʉ nek jeh pia-saa a-vwey klah?
           តើ អ្នក ចេះ ភាសា អ្វី ខ្លះ
           What languages do you know?

        B: kñom jeh pia-saa ɔng-glee nəng pia-saa kmae.
           ខ្ញុំ ចេះ ភាសា អង់គ្លេស និង ភាសា ខ្មែរ
           I know English and Cambodian.

9.   A: dtaʉ bɔɔng jeh sɔɔ-see ak-sɔɔ jen dtee?
           តើ បង ចេះ សរសេរ អក្សរ ចិន ទេ
           Do you know how to write Chinese?

        B: baat, kñom jeh sɔɔ-see ak-sɔɔ jen.
           បាទ ខ្ញុំ ចេះ សរសេរ អក្សរ ចិន
           Yes, I can write Chinese.

        C: dtee, kñom min jeh sɔɔ-see ak-sɔɔ jen dtee.
           ទេ ខ្ញុំ មិន ចេះ សរសេរ អក្សរ ចិន ទេ
           No, I don't know how to write Chinese.

        D. kñom jeh sɔɔ-see ak-sɔɔ jen bɔn-dtek-bɔn-dtuuik.
           ខ្ញុំ ចេះ សរសេរ អក្សរ ចិន បន្តិចបន្តួច
           I can write a little Chinese.

Note: 1. A simple answer of *baan* to a yes-no question literally means "You
           may" or "It is possible." However, in the sentences above,
           alternate figurative meanings could be "That's all right" or
           "That's fine."

Drills

1. Practice asking and answering the following questions in Cambodian.

Where are you going?

_____

Can I go see a movie?

_____

May I please speak in English?

_____

Do you know how to speak Cambodian?

_____

2. Write a dialogue between two people that includes at least one of the following.

A discussion between two people asking what they want to do and where they want to go.

Asking permission to do something.

Asking someone if they can speak a certain language and if they can write in that language.

Use the following words to help form ten sentences.

kmae	dtəɥ	jeh	mon-dtii-bpeet
kñom	baan	a-vwey	vial-yun-hɔh
goat	dtiñ	ni-yiay	haang-jak-sang
dtee	rian	nəɥ	məəl
soom	ak-sɔɔ	pleeng	geeng
jen	gee	aaik	leeng
dtaɥ	jool-jet	ɔng-glee	pia-saa
gee-laa	ga-boob	siaw-pəɥ	jɔng

Test 3

Match the English words with the Cambodian words.

_____ 1. hospital

_____ 2. to go

_____ 3. to buy

_____ 4. market

_____ 5. music

_____ 6. alphabet

_____ 7. to play

_____ 8. to like, prefer

_____ 9. bank

_____ 10. can

_____ 11. possible

_____ 12. movie

a. dtiñ ទិញ

b. jool-jet ចូលចិត្ត

c. gon កុន

d. to-nia-gia ធនាគារ

e. mon-dtii-bpeet មន្ទីរពេទ្យ

f. baan បាន

g. ak-sɔɔ អក្សរ

h. ñam ញ៉ាំ

i. məəl មើល

j. psaa ផ្សារ

k. aaik អាច

l. leng លេង

m. dtəɥ ទៅ

n. vwial-yun-hɔh វាលយន្តហោះ

o. pleeng ភ្លេង

Translate the following into English or Cambodian.

1. kñom jeh sɔɔ-see ak-sɔɔ jo-bpun.

    ខ្ញុំ ចេះ សរសេរ អក្សរ ជប៉ុន

    _____

2. kñom soom dtəu bɔn-dtub-dtək baan dtee?

    ខ្ញុំ សូម ទៅ បន្ទប់ទឹក បាន ទេ

    _____

3. goat jɔng dtəu leeng bal.

    គាត់ ចង់ ទៅ លេង បាល់

    _____

4. He is going to study at the library.

    _____

5. May I please go watch a movie?

    _____

Consonants ព្យញ្ជនៈ pjuañ-jiah-nɛa

Here are eight more consonants in the Cambodian alphabet. These consonants are also a mixture the of /ɔɔ/ and /oo/ consonant classes.

Consonant	Pronunciation	Sound
ប	bɔɔ	/b/[1]
ផ	pɔɔ	/p/
ព	bpoo	/bp/
ភ	poo	/p/
ម	moo	/m/
យ	yoo	/y/
រ	roo	/r/
ល	loo	/l/

Note: 1. When *sra aa* (ា) is added to bɔɔ (ប) the combined new character set becomes បា for *baa*.   This is because the normal combination would make the បា character which could be easily confused with the character hɔɔ (ហ). For this reason, an alternate character set was developed. Also, when ប is combined with *sra au* (ៅ) or *sra ao* (ៅ), it respectively forms បៅ or បៅ in this same manner.

Practice Writing Consonants

Practice writing the following consonants. Remember to use the proper stroke order as shown below.

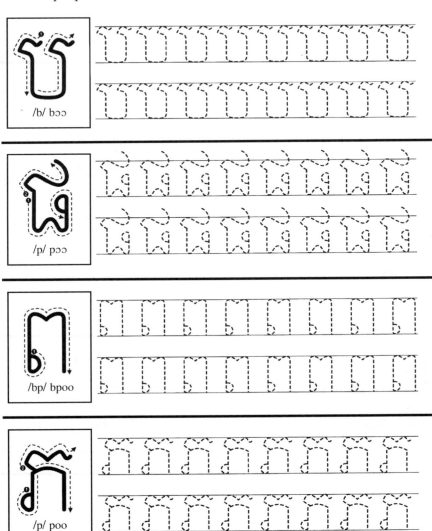

/b/ bɔɔ

/p/ pɔɔ

/bp/ bpoo

/p/ poo

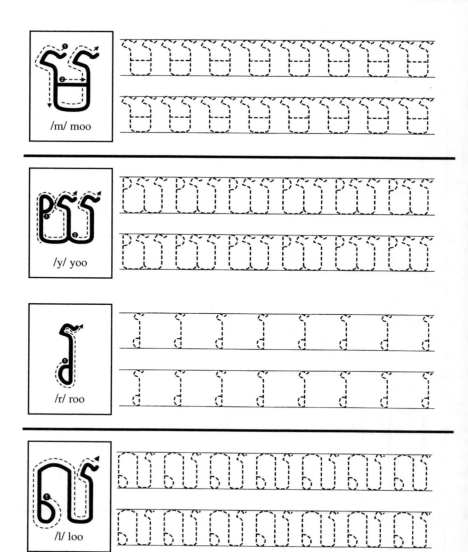

/m/ moo

/y/ yoo

/r/ roo

/l/ loo

More Vowels ស្រៈ sra

The following vowels are the next six vowels in the Cambodian alphabet. Remember to distinguish between the /ɔɔ/ and /oo/ consonant classes when forming vowel sounds.

Vowel	Vowel Name	Sound /ɔɔ/-/oo/
ៅ-ា	sra ao	/ao/-/oo/
ៅ-ៅ	sra au	/au/-/əɨ/
ំ	sra om	/om/-/um/
ំ	sra ɔm	/ɔm/-/əm/
ាំ	sra am	/am/-/oam/
ាំង	—	/ang/-/ɛang/[1]

Note: 1. This vowel is actually not listed as a vowel in the Cambodian alphabet because it is simply a *sra am* with a *ngoo* on the end. However, it does have a completely different vowel sound than what this phonetic combination would suggest. For that reason, it is listed in this book as a seperate vowel.

Practice Writing the Following Vowels

Use ក /-/ as the consonant when practicing the following vowels.

កោ   កោ   កោ   កោ

កៅ   កៅ   កៅ   កៅ

កុំ   កុំ   កុំ   កុំ

កំ   កំ   កំ   កំ

កាំ   កាំ   កាំ   កាំ

កាំង   កាំង   កាំង   កាំង

Read The Following Aloud

1. បោ បៅ បុំ បំ បាំ បាំង

2. ផោ ផៅ ផុំ ផំ ផាំ ផាំង

3. ពោ ពៅ ពុំ ពំ ពាំ ពាំង

4. ភោ ភៅ ភុំ ភំ ភាំ ភាំង

5. មោ មៅ មុំ មំ មាំ មាំង

6. យោ យៅ យុំ យំ យាំ យាំង

7. រោ រៅ រុំ រំ រាំ រាំង

8. លោ លៅ លុំ លំ លាំ លាំង

Reading Exercise: Read the following words and practice writing them in Cambodian.

1. ក្រោ   youngest child

2. រាំ   to dance

3. យំ   to cry

4. រាំង   dry, without rain

5. លើ   above

6. មេ   leader

7. ចៅ   grandchildren

8. ពុំ   not (formal)

9. គោ   ox, cow

10. បៀ   playing cards

11. មាំ   firm, stable

12. ធំ   big

Final Consonants

Final consonant sounds in Cambodian are very similar to their English equivalents. A final consonant emits its natural consonant sound without its accompanying vowel sound.

e.g. ខាង = *kaang* (not *kaa-ngoo*)

Not all the consonants in the Cambodian alphabet are commonly used as final consonants. Below are some of the most common final consonants and their respective final consonant sounds.

ក /-k/[1]   ង /-ng/   ញ /-ñ/   ត /-t/[2]

ន /-n/   ប /-b/[3]   ម /-m/   ល /-l/

Less common final consonants include the following:

ខ /-k/[1]   គ /-k/[1]   ដ /-t/[2]   ណ /-n/   ថ /-t/[2]

ជ /-t/[2]   ឆ /-t/[2]   ព /-b/[3]   ភ /-b/[3]

Some final consonants do not emit their natural consonant sound. For example, a យ *yoo* does not have a final /y/ sound when it is used as a final consonant. Instead, it is more like an /ii/ sound. Don't worry! English is no different. Just think of a final /y/ sound in the word "soy" or "buy." Cambodian is the same. Another important exception is រ *roo*. If this letter is the final consonant, the letter is silent as if there was no final consonant at all. These and other exception final consonants are listed below.

យ /-ii/   ថ /-ik/   ជ /-ik/   រ /-silent/   ស /-h/4   វ /-w/4

Note: 1. Even though these consonants may have different consonant sounds, they all have a virtually identical /k/ final consonant sound.
2..Even though these consonants may have different consonant sounds, they all have a virtually identical /t/ final consonant sound.
3. Even though these consonants may have different consonant sounds, they all have a virtually identical /b/ final consonant sound.
4. These consonants will be introduced in the next chapter.

Reading Exercise: The following words have final consonant sounds. Practice reading and writing them in Cambodian.

1. កាល	period of time	2. យាយ	grandmother
3. រៀន	to study	4. កើត	to be born
5. លើក	to lift	6. មួយ	one
7. ចាប	bird	8. យូរ	long
9. ខូច	broken	10. រឿង	story
11. តាម	to follow	12. ទិញ	to buy
13. ចោល	to throw away	14. ដែក	metal

Writing Exercise 3

Transcribe the following into Cambodian script. There may be several ways to phonetically spell some of the words. If necessary, remember to use the appropriate final consonant. Try to use the most common final consonants as shown on pages 80-81.

1. juab _____

2. rum _____

3. laan _____

4. jaan _____

5. bəng _____

6. nəʉ _____

7. dtiñ _____

8. dteang _____

9. sɔɔm _____

10. niang _____

11. gul _____

12. yiay _____

13. jɔɔng _____

14. lia _____

15. gaot _____

16. chiang _____

17. jɔm _____

18. juut _____

19. dom _____

20. lʉan _____

Lesson 4

jeh, dəng, and *sgoal* (to know); *bpon-maan* (how much, how many); modifiers; more vowels and consonants

mee-rian dtii buan មេរៀន ទី៤   Lesson 4
vɛak-a-sab   វាក្យសព្ទ   Vocabulary

sgoal	ស្គាល់	to know of, recognize
dəng	ដឹង	to know
pləшw	ផ្លូវ	road, path
aa-saay-a-taan	អាស័យដ្ឋាន	address
leek dtuu-re-sab	លេខទូរស័ព្ទ	phone number
taa	ថា	that
bpuak-maak	ពួកម៉ាក	friend
grua-saa	គ្រួសារ	family
bpon-dtae	ប៉ុន្តែ	but
haшy	ហើយ	already
bpon-maan	ប៉ុន្មាន	how much, how many
rial	រៀល	riel (Cambodian currency); dollar
dol-laa	ដុល្លារ	dollar
gak	កាក់	one-tenth of a riel
chnam	ឆ្នាំ	year
kae	ខែ	month
aa-yu	អាយុ	age
muay naa	មួយណា	which one
nek naa	អ្នកណា	anyone, who
yook	យក	to take
daш	ដើរ	to walk
tlai	ថ្លៃ	expensive
taok	ថោក	cheap
nah	ណាស់	very, much
jraшn	ច្រើន	many, a lot

tom ធំ	big
dtooik តូច	small
lmoom ល្មម	enough, just right
lʉan លឿន	fast
yʉʉt យឺត	slow
laan ឡាន	car
vwɛɛng វែង	long (length)
yuu យូរ	long (time)
kley ខ្លី	short
lɔ-ɔɔ ល្អ	good
aa-grɔk អាក្រក់	bad[1]
rəng រឹង	hard
dton ទន់	soft
jit ជិត	near
chngaay ឆ្ងាយ	far
bpeek ពេក	too (as in "too much")
bpoa ពណ៌	color
(bpoa) grɔ-hɔɔm (ពណ៌)ក្រហម	red
(bpoa) kiaw (ពណ៌)ខៀវ	blue/green[2]
(bpoa) bai-dtɔɔng (ពណ៌)បៃតង	green[2]
(bpoa) lʉang (ពណ៌)លឿង	yellow
(bpoa) tnaot (ពណ៌)ត្នោត	brown
(bpoa) kmau (ពណ៌)ខ្មៅ	black
(bpoa) sɔɔ (ពណ៌)ស	white
aa-nih អានេះ	this one
aa-nuh អានោះ	that one
aa-tom អាធំ	the big one
aa-dtooik អាតូច	the small one

Note: 1. *aa-krɔk* is a very harsh word and should only be used when the word
          "bad" is used in a very harsh context. For other situations, it
          is more appropriate to use *min lɔ-ɔɔ* or *ɔt lɔ-ɔɔ* which means
          "not good."
       2. Many students of Cambodian find it odd that the word *kiaw* means
          either blue or green. Apparently Cambodians don't see a need
          to distinguish between the two. If it is absloutely necessary to
          distinguish between the two, the word *bai-dtɔɔng* can be used
          for green, but this word is rarely used in common speech.

Note on Cambodian Monetary System

Cambodia's monetary system is very complicated. The national currency is the
Khmer riel. However, due to fears of inflation, Cambodia has also adopted the
U.S. dollar as a favorite currency, and both are used together. To make things
even more complicated, dollars are commonly called riel. However, at the time
this book went to press, one dollar is equal to approximately 3800 riel, so the difference is easy to distinguish. Hypothetically, if you were given a price of *bey
rial bpii kak*, that would mean three dollars and two tenths of one dollar (760
riel). However, the smallest common denominator is 100 Riel so you have to
round up or down. You would pay by providing the desired amount in both cur-
rencies (three dollars, 800 riel). If you just gave them four dollars, they would
give you 3000 riel in change. Cambodia does not currently use coin money, so
don't try to use U.S. change. It can be very complicated to figure all of this out,
so if you are not good at math, don't forget your calculator!

vwee-jia-gɔɔ វេយ្យាករណ៍ Grammar

You have already learned one form of the word "to know." This is the word *jeh* which means "to know how to do." Cambodian has two separate words for other forms of the English word "know." The first word is *dəng* which means to know something or to have knowledge of something.

e.g. kñom dəng. = I know.
kñom min dəng dtee. = I don't know.

The word *taa* is also commonly added after the word *dəng* to form the phrase "know that."

e.g. kñom dəng taa goat nəʉ pdtɛah. = I know that he is at home.

The second word is the word *sgoal*. This means to "know of."

e.g. dtaʉ look sgoal bɔɔng Tim dtee? = Do you know Tim?

bpon-maan is a very useful Cambodian word. It is commonly used in combination with the word *tlai* to form the phrase "how much." The word is also almost always used at the end of the sentence.

e.g. aa-nih tlai bpon-maan? = How much is this one?
(Literally: This one expensive how much?)

However, *bpon-maan* can also mean "how many" when followed by a classifier.

e.g. dtaʉ bɔɔng mian luy bpon-maan rial? =
How many riel do you have?
(Literally: You have money how many riel?)

bpon-maan can also mean "that much."

e.g. pia-saa kmae min bpi-baak bpon-maan dtee. =
Cambodian is not that difficult.
(Literally: Cambodian not difficult that much.)

This chapter also includes a basic introduction on Cambodian modifiers. In general, a modifier comes after the word it modifies. Again, the "to be" verb *jia* is not used between a word and a modifier.

e.g. laan tom = big car

laan nih tom.   = This car is big.
(Literally: Car this big.)

jia can be used in sentences with modifiers only if it is used in the standard subject-verb-object sentence structure.
nih jia laan tom. = This is a big car.
(Literally: This is car big.)

Verbs are modified in the same way as nouns.
e.g. ni-yiay luan = speak fast
goat dau yuut. = He walks slowly.
(Literally: He walk slow.)

It is important to understand the difference between the modifiers *nah* and *jraun*. *nah* modifies adjectives or adverbs while *jraun* modifies nouns or verbs. *nah* can also modify *jraun* in the same sentence in order to provide extra emphasis.
e.g. laan nih luan nah. = This car is very fast.
goat ni-yiay jraun. = He talks a lot.
look mian siaw-pəu jraun. = You have a lot of books.
look mian siaw-pəu jraun nah. = You have tons of books!

This chapter also teaches a new meaning of the word *hauy*. *hauy* can also mean "already" and is used very frequently in Cambodian speech at the end of a sentence.
e.g. gee jeh ni-yiay hauy. = He already knows how to talk.
(Literally: He knows how to talk already.)
kñom məəl gon nih hauy. = I've already seen this movie.
hauy is also commonly used to as a word to indentfy past tense. As discussed earlier, Cambodian usually does not show tenses through verb conjugation. Instead, tense is often understood through context or other identifying words. *hauy* is one of these words. Tenses will be discussed in more detail in Chapter 5.
e.g. kñom dtəu psaa hauy. = I went to the store.
(Literally: I go store already.)

<u>**Conversation 1**</u>

Bob: kñom jɔng dtəɰ məəl gon.
បប ខ្ញុំ ចង់ ទៅ មើល កុន
I want to go watch a movie.

Sopha: kñom jɔng dtəɰ məəl dae, bpon-dtae kñom min
sgoal roong-gon muay naa nəɰ jit nih dtee.[1]
សុផា ខ្ញុំ ចង់ ទៅ មើល ដែរ ប៉ុន្តែ ខ្ញុំ មិន
ស្គាល់ រោងកុន មួយ ណា នៅ ជិត នេះ ទេ
I also want to go, but I don't know of a movie
theater near here.

Bob: nəɰ pləɰw nih mian roong-gon tom muay.
បប នៅ ផ្លូវ នេះ មាន រោងកុន ធំ មួយ
This street has a big movie theater.

Sopha: roong-gon nuh nəɰ jit rɰɰ chngaay?
សុផា រោងកុន នោះ នៅ ជិត ឬ ឆ្ងាយ
Is that theater close by or far away?

Bob: nəɰ jit. jɔng dtəɰ dtee?[2]
បប នៅ ជិត ចង់ ទៅ ទេ
It's close by. Do you want to go?

Sopha: jaa, kñom jɔng dtəɰ.
សុផា ចាំ ខ្ញុំ ចង់ ទៅ
Yes, I want to go.

Notes: 1. *muay naa* means "which one," but it can also mean the rough
equivalent of the English article "a."
2. Notice how the subject is omitted in both sentences. This is very
common in colloquial speech.

<u>Conversation 2</u>

Kim: aa-nih tlai bpon-maan?
យិម   អានេះ ថ្លៃ ប៉ុន្មាន
                How much is this one?

Vendor: bpii rial bpram gak.
អ្នកលក់   ពីរ រៀល ប្រាំ កាក់
                Two dollars and fifty cents.

Kim: tlai nah. joh, aa-nuh tlai bpon-maan dae?
យិម   ថ្លៃ ណាស់ ចុះ អានោះ ថ្លៃ ប៉ុន្មាន ដែរ
                Oh, that's expensive. Well, how much is that one.

Vendor: aa-nuh muay rial.
អ្នកលក់   អានោះ មួយ រៀល
                That one is one dollar.

Kim: taok dae. kñom yook muay.
យិម   ថោក ដែរ ខ្ញុំ យក មួយ
                That's cheap. I'll take one.

klia ឃ្លា Sentences

1. A: dtaʉ bɔɔng sgoal goat dtee?
   តើ បង ស្គាល់ គាត់ ទេ
   Do you know him?

   B: kñom sgoal.
   ខ្ញុំ ស្គាល់
   I know him.

   C: kñom min sgoal goat dtee.
   ខ្ញុំ មិន ស្គាល់ គាត់ ទេ
   I don't know him.

2. A: dtaʉ look sgoal nek naa klah?
   តើ លោក ស្គាល់ អ្នក ណា ខ្លះ
   Who do you know?

   B: kñom sgoal bɔɔng so-paa bɔɔng tim haʉy-nəng bɔɔng so-kaa.[1]
   ខ្ញុំ ស្គាល់ បង សុផា បង ធិម ហើយនិង
   បង សុខា
   I know Sopha, Tim, and Sokha.

   C: kñom min sgoal nek naa dtee.
   ខ្ញុំ មិន ស្គាល់ អ្នក ណា ទេ
   I don't know anybody.

3. A: dtaʉ bɔɔng sgoal leek dtuu-re-sab kñom dtee?
   តើ បង ស្គាល់ លេខ ទូរស័ព្ទ ខ្ញុំ ទេ
   Do you know my phone number?

   B: sgoal.
   ស្គាល់
   Yes.

   C: ɔt/min sgoal dtee.
   អត់/មិន ស្គាល់ ទេ
   No.

4. A: dtaʉ goat mook bpii naa?
   តើ គាត់ មក ពី ណា
   Where is she from?

B: kñom min dəng dtee.

ខ្ញុំ មិន ដឹង ទេ

I don't know.

C: kñom dəng taa goat mook bpii pnom-bpeeñ.

ខ្ញុំ ដឹង ថា គាត់ មក ពី ភ្នំពេញ

I know that she is from Phnom Penh.

5.   A: dtaʉ bɔɔng mian laan bpon-maan?[2]

តើ បង មាន ឡាន ប៉ុន្មាន

How many cars do you have?

B: kñom mian laan bpii.

ខ្ញុំ មាន ឡាន ពីរ

I have two cars.

6.   A: dtaʉ bɔɔng mian luy bpon-maan rial.[2]

តើ បង មាន លុយ ប៉ុន្មាន រៀល

How many dollars do you have?

B: kñom mian bey rial.

ខ្ញុំ មាន បី រៀល

I have three dollars.

7.   A: dtaʉ look rian pia-saa kmae bpon-maan chnam haʉy?

តើ លោក រៀន ភាសា ខ្មែរ ប៉ុន្មាន ឆ្នាំ ហើយ

How many years have you been studying Cambodian?

B: kñom rian muay chnam haʉy.

ខ្ញុំ រៀន មួយ ឆ្នាំ ហើយ

I have been learning for one year.

8.   A: ɔt-dtooh. dtaʉ bɔɔng aa-yu bpon-maan?

អត់ទោស តើ បង អាយុ ប៉ុន្មាន

Excuse me. How old are you?

B: kñom aa-yu mpei-bpram chnam.

ខ្ញុំ អាយុ ម្ភៃប្រាំ ឆ្នាំ

I am twenty-five years old.

9.   A: goat ɔt jeh ɔng-glee bpon-maan dtee.

គាត់ អត់ ចេះ អង់គ្លេស ប៉ុន្មាន ទេ

He doesn't know that much English.

10. goat mian luy jraʉn.
គាត់ មាន លុយ ច្រើន
He has a lot of money.

11. pdtɛah nuh tom nah.
ផ្ទះ នោះ ធំ ណាស់
That house very so big.

12. goat jeh kmae jraʉn nah.
គាត់ ចេះ ខ្មែរ ច្រើន ណាស់
She knows so much Cambodian!

13. A: dtaʉ look jɔng baan bpon-maan?
តើ លោក ចង់ បាន ប៉ុន្មាន
How much do you want?

B: kñom jɔng baan jraʉn.
ខ្ញុំ ចង់ បាន ច្រើន
I want a lot.

14. goat ni-yiay jraʉn.
គាត់ និយាយ ច្រើន
He talks a lot.

15. kñom dtəʉ psaa haʉy.
ខ្ញុំ ទៅ ផ្សារ ហើយ
I already went to the store.

16. goat mian laan haʉy.
គាត់ មាន ឡាន ហើយ
He already has a car.

17. A: pdtɛah goat nəʉ chngaay.
ផ្ទះ គាត់ នៅ ឆ្ងាយ
His house is far away.

B: pdtɛah goat nəʉ jit.
ផ្ទះ គាត់ នៅ ជិត
His house is close by.

18. A: grɛɛ nih rəng nah.
គ្រែ នេះ រឹង ណាស់
This bed is very hard.

B: grɛɛ nih dton nah.
គ្រែ នេះ ទន់ ណាស់
This bed is very soft.

19. A: aa-nih dtooik bpeek.
អានេះ តូច ពេក
This one is too small.

B: aa-nih tom bpeek.
អានេះ ធំ ពេក
This one is too big.

20: laan nih luan nah, bpon-dtae knŏm min jɔng dtiñ vwia dtee.
ឡាន នេះ លឿន ណាស់ ប៉ុន្តែ ខ្ញុំ មិន ចង់ ទិញ វា ទេ
This car is very fast, but I don't want to buy it.

21. pia-saa jen srual rian, bpon-dtae kñom ɔt jeh dtee.
ភាសា ចិន ស្រួល រៀន ប៉ុន្តែ ខ្ញុំ អត់ ចេះ ទេ
Chinese is easy to learn, but I don't know it.

22. gon nih lɔ-ɔɔ məəl. kñom jɔng dtəu məəl vwia.
កុន នេះ ល្អ មើល ខ្ញុំ ចង់ ទៅ មើល វា
This movie is good. I want to go see it.

Notes: 1. In this sentence, the word *bɔɔng* is used as a prefix placed before the names of individuals not participating in the conversation. This is very common in Cambodian speech. This indicates that these individuals are either older than the speaker or friends with the speaker. The word *look* can be used in the same manner when speaking of individuals who are much older or of a high social status.

2. When you are asking "how many," use the word *bpon-maan* after the object you are trying to account for.
e.g. *pdtɛah bpon-maan?* = How many homes?
However, if you are asking "how many" with a classifier, then the classifier should be placed after *bpon-maan*. More Cambodian classifiers will be introduced in later chapters.
e.g. *bpon-maan dol-laa?* = How many dollars?

Drills

1. Practice saying the following sentences in Cambodian. If it is a question, practice answering it as well.

I know that the market is close by.

_____

How old is John?

_____

I want to go to Thailand, but I don't speak Thai.

_____

2. Do at least one of the following:

Write a two person dialogue describing how much something is and if it is cheap or expensive.

Write a paragraph describing your car. You must use at least three modifiers.

Write six sentences, using *jeh, dəng,* and *sgoal.* Use each word twice.

3. Use the following words to help form ten sentences.

bɔɔng	so-paa	laan
aa-nih	tom	sgoal
grua-saa	pdtɛah	jit
bpeek	tlai	bpon-dtae
jɔng	kñom	chngaay
rial	taok	bpii
nih	dtooik	dtaʉ
nəʉ	dəng	taa
mian	nah	jraʉn
bpon-maan	min	luy

Test 4

Match the English words with the Cambodian words.

_____ 1. far   a. sgoal ស្គាល់

_____ 2. soft   b. grua-saa គ្រួសារ

_____ 3. family   c. aa-yu អាយុ

_____ 4. road   d. chngaay ឆ្ងាយ

_____ 5. cheap   e. bpon-dtae ប៉ុន្ដែ

_____ 6. telephone number   f. kae ខែ

_____ 7. short   g. lmoom ល្មម

_____ 8. month   h. kley ខ្លី

_____ 9. to know of, recognize   i. vwɛɛng វែង

_____ 10. very   j. jraʉn ច្រើន

_____ 11. age   k. dəng ដឹង

_____ 12. a lot   l. taok ថោក

_____ 13. to know something   m. rəng រឹង

_____ 14. long   o. pləʉw ផ្លូវ

                     p. dton ទន់

                     q. leek dtuu-re-sab លេខទូរស័ព្ទ

                     r. nah ណាស់

Word Exercise

Insert the correct form of the word "to know" (*jeh, dəng,* or *sgoal*) in the following sentences. You may need to add the word *taa* after *dəng.*

1. kñom _____ laan nih tlai.

   ខ្ញុំ _____ ឡាន នេះ ថ្លៃ

2. goat _____ ni-yiay pia-saa jen.

   គាត់ _____ និយាយ ភាសា ចិន

3. bɔɔng so-paa _____ pdtɛah kñom.

   បង សុផា _____ ផ្ទះ ខ្ញុំ

4. kñom min _____ vial-yon-hɔh nəɯ jit nih dtee

   ខ្ញុំ មិន _____ វាលយន្តហោះ នៅ ជិត នេះ ទេ

5. kñom _____ goat jeh pia-saa jraɯn.

   ខ្ញុំ _____ គាត់ ចេះ ភាសា ច្រើន

6. so-pia _____ leeng pleeng bɔn-dtik-bɔn-dtuiik.

   សុភា _____ លេង ភ្លេង បន្តិចបន្តួច

Consonants ព្យញ្ជនៈ pjuñ-jia-nea

Here are the final eight consonants in the Cambodian alphabet. These consonants are also a mixture the of /ɔɔ/ and /oo/ consonant classes.

Consonant	Pronunciation	Sound
វ៉	vwoo	/vw/
ស៉	sɔɔ	/s/
ហា	hɔɔ	/h/
ឡ៉	lɔɔ	/l/
អ	ɔɔ	/ɔɔ/
ប៉	tɔɔ	/t/[1]
ឌ	doo	/d/[1]
ញ៉	too	/t/[1]

Note: 1. These three consonants are obselete and rarely used.

Practice Writing Consonants

Practice writing the following consonants. Remember to use the proper stroke order as shown below.

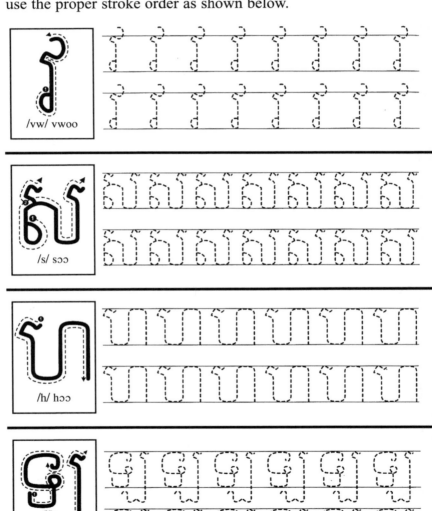

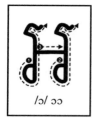 /ɔ/ cɔ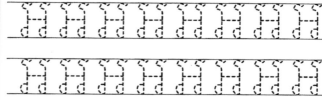

 /t/ tɔɔ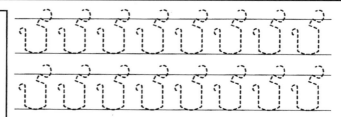

 /d/ doo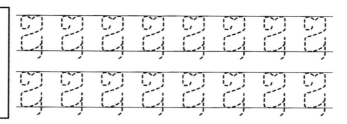

 /t/ too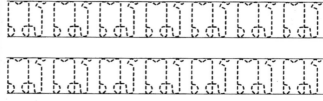

More Vowels ស្រៈ sra

The following vowels are the final vowels in the Cambodian alphabet. Remember to distinguish between the /ɔɔ/ and /oo/ consonant classes when forming vowel sounds.

Vowel	Vowel Name	Sound /ɔɔ/-/oo/
-ះ	sra ah	/ah/-/ɛah/
-ឹះ	sra eh	/eh/-/ih/[1]
-ុះ	sra oh	/oh/-/uh/
េ-ះ	sra eh	/eh/-/ih/[1]
េ-ាះ	sra ɔh	/ɔh/-/uah/[2]

Notes: 1. These two vowels produce identical sounds, but the second one is much more common.

2. Sometimes /oo/ series consonants can also produce an /uh/ sound with this vowel.

Practice Writing the Following Vowels

Use ក /-/ as the consonant when practicing the following vowels.

Read the Following Aloud

1. វៈ វិៈ វុៈ វេៈ វាៈ

2. សៈ សិៈ សុៈ សេៈ សាៈ

3. ហៈ ហិៈ ហុៈ ហេៈ ហាៈ

4. ឡៈ ឡិៈ ឡុៈ ឡេៈ ឡាៈ

5. អៈ អិៈ អុៈ អេៈ អាៈ

6. បៈ បិៈ បុៈ បេៈ បាៈ

7. ខៈ ខិៈ ខុៈ ខេៈ ខាៈ

8. ឈៈ ឈិៈ ឈុៈ ឈេៈ ឈាៈ

Reading Exercise: Read the following words and practice writing them in Cambodian.

1. ទះ — to slap

2. ហោះ — to fly

3. ឡើង — to rise

4. ជិះ — to ride

5. សេះ — horse

6. វះ — to operate

7. កោះ — island

8. ចុះ — to descend

9. វាល — a field

10. អាវ — shirt

11. ចេះ — to know how to do something

12. បាន — place

Writing Exercise 4

Transcribe the following into Cambodian script. These are all real Cambodian words. However, you may be able to phonetically spell them several different ways.

1. saab _____

2. lauy _____

3. reah _____

4. haam _____

5. bpuah _____

6. bɔh _____

7. aa _____

8. nih _____

9. huah _____

10. geh _____

11. vwia _____

12. dɔh _____

13. beh _____

14. leah _____

15. aaik _____

16. saen _____

17. jih _____

18. luh _____

19. liang _____

20. hau _____

Lesson 5

Tenses; telling time; *jəəng* lowercase script introduced; independent vowels

mee-rian dtii bpram   មេរៀន ទី៥   Lesson 5

veak-a-sab   វាក្យសព្ទ   Vocabulary

bpeel/vwee-lia ពេល/វេលា	time; when[1]
bpeel-bprək/bprək/bprək bpro-ləm ពេលព្រឹក/ព្រឹក/ព្រឹកព្រលឹម	morning
bpeel-ro-sial/ro-sial/tngai-dtrɔng ពេលរសៀល/រសៀល/ថ្ងៃត្រង់	afternoon
bpeel-lngiak/lngiak/ ពេលល្ងាច / ល្ងាច	evening
bpeel-yub/yub/ria-dtrey ពេលយប់/យប់/រាត្រី	night
maong ម៉ោង	hour, o'clock
nia-dtii នាទី	minute
vwi-nia-dtii វិនាទី	second
gɔn-lah កន្លះ	half
dtiat ទៀត	more
dɔl ដល់	at, to arrive
bpii/dtang-bpii ពី / តាំងពី	from, since, ever since
ɔng-gaal អង្កាល	when (future)
bpii ɔng-gaal ពីអង្កាល	when (past)
juab ជួប	to meet
juay ជួយ	to help
jab-pdaum ចាប់ផ្ដើម	to start, begin
jɔb ចប់	to end
jia-muay ជាមួយ	with
knia គ្នា	together
baan បាន	past tense identifier[2]
gɔm-bpung កំពុង	present tense identifier[2]
nəng នឹង	future tense identifier[2]

bpeel-vee-lia ពេលវេលា Time

maong-bpon-maan (haɯy) ម៉ោងប៉ុន្មាន (ហើយ)			What time is it?
am	12:00	maong-dɔb-bpii/aa-dtriat	ម៉ោងដប់ពីរ / អធ្រាត្រ
	1:00	maong-muay (gɔn-lɔɔng aa-dtriat)	ម៉ោងមួយ (កន្លងអធ្រាត្រ)
	2:00	maong-bpii (gɔn-lɔɔng aa-dtriat)	ម៉ោងពីរ (កន្លងអធ្រាត្រ)
	3:00	maong-bey (plɯɯ)	ម៉ោងបី (ភ្លឺ)³
	4:00	maong-buan (plɯɯ)	ម៉ោងបួន (ភ្លឺ)
	5:00	maong-bpram (bprək)	ម៉ោងប្រាំ (ព្រឹក)
	6:00	maong-bpram-muay (bprək)	ម៉ោងប្រាំមួយ (ព្រឹក)
	7:00	maong-bpram-bpii (bprək)/ maong-bpram-bpəl (bprək)	ម៉ោងប្រាំពីរ (ព្រឹក)/ ម៉ោងប្រាំពីល (ព្រឹក)
	8:00	maong-bpram-bey (bprək)	ម៉ោងប្រាំបី (ព្រឹក)
	9:00	maong-bpram-buan (bprək)	ម៉ោងប្រាំបួន (ព្រឹក)
	10:00	maong-dɔb (bprək)	ម៉ោងដប់ (ព្រឹក)
	11:00	maong-dɔb-muay (bprək)	ម៉ោងដប់មួយ (ព្រឹក)
pm	12:00	maong-dɔb-bpii/ tngai dtrɔng	ម៉ោងដប់ពីរ / ថ្ងៃត្រង់
	1:00	maong-muay (ro-sial)	ម៉ោងមួយ (រសៀល)
	2:00	maong-bpii (ro-sial)	ម៉ោងពីរ (រសៀល)
	3:00	maong-bey (ro-sial)	ម៉ោងបី (រសៀល)
	4:00	maong-buan (ro-sial)	ម៉ោងបួន (រសៀល)
	5:00	maong-bpram (lngiak)	ម៉ោងប្រាំ (ល្ងាច)
	6:00	maong-bpram-muay (lngiak)	ម៉ោងប្រាំមួយ (ល្ងាច)
	7:00	maong-bpram-bpii (lngiak)/ maong-bpram-bpəl (lngiak)	ម៉ោងប្រាំពីរ (ល្ងាច)/ ម៉ោងប្រាំពីល (ល្ងាច)
	8:00	maong-bpram-bey (yub)	ម៉ោងប្រាំបី (យប់)
	9:00	maong-bpram-buan (yub)	ម៉ោងប្រាំបួន (យប់)
	10:00	maong-dɔb (yub)	ម៉ោងដប់ (យប់)
	11:00	maong-dɔb-muay (yub)	ម៉ោងដប់មួយ (យប់)

Note: 1. *vwee-lia* is more formal than *bpeel*. However, the two can also be used to form the combination word *bpeel-vee-lia* in some circumstances.

2. Please see the section on tenses on page 114 for more details.

3. *pluu, bprək, ro-sial,* and *lngiak* only need to be added to a certain time of day when the context of the conversation does not already reveal this information. For example, if someone asks you when you get up, and you want to reply that you get up at 6:00, you do not need to add the word *bprək* to your answer because it is already assumed from the context of the question that you get up in the morningtime.

vwee-jia-gɔɔ   វេយ្យាករណ៍   **Grammar**

The main purpose of this chapter is to teach how to express time in Cambodian. Telling time in Cambodian is actually very simple! The phrase *maong bpon-maan haʉy* literally means "hour how many already." All that is required for an answer is the word *maong* followed by whatever number is required. Usually *haʉy* is added to the answer as well to show that it is already that time.

e.g. maong bpon-maan haʉy? = What time is it?
maong bey (haʉy). = It's three o'clock (already).

When asking a question regarding a time in the future, *haʉy* is obviously dropped.

e.g. jɔng dtəʉ maong bpon-maan? = What time do you want to go?
jɔng dtəʉ maong buan. = I want to go at 4:00.

As you can probably already tell from our earlier lesson, the phrase *bpon-maan maong* means "how many hours." It can also figuratively mean "how long," and it is always used at the end of the sentence.

e.g. bɔɔng nəʉ pdtɛah bpon-maan maong? =
"How many hours were you at home?" Or figuratively, "How long were you at home?"

When expressing times which do not fall exactly on the hour, all you have to do is add the number of minutes after the time.

e.g. 4:25 = maong-buan mpei-bpram ni-dtii.

The only exception is the half hour where the word *gɔn-lah* is used.

e.g. 9:30 = maong-bpram-buan gɔn-lah.

It is also important to note that you reverse the word order to show an amount of hours. Two o'clock would be *maong-bpii*, but two hours would be *bpii maong*.

The word *bpii,* or *dtang-bpii,* roughly means "since" or "ever since."
e.g. goat nəu nih dtang-bpii maong bpram bprək. =
He's been here since 5:00 am.

bpii can also be used in combination with *ɔng-gaal* which means "when." When the word *bpii* is added to the beginning of *ɔng-gaal,* this indicates that "when" means "when in the past." If *bpii* is omitted and *ɔng-gaal* is left by itself, this means "when in the future." *ɔng-gaal* and *bpii ɔng-gaal* are always used at the end of a sentence. Both of these words are also examples of words that imply a tense through context.
e.g. goat dtəu bpii ɔng-gaal? = When did she go?
goat dtəu ɔng-gaal? = When will she go?
goat mook nih bpii ɔng-gaal? = When did she come here?

The word *bpeel* can be used to make the non-question equivalent of the word "when." Sometimes the word *nəu* is added before *bpeel* to form the phrase *nəu bpeel.* This literally means "at the time." Many Cambodians also use the word *gaal* for the the word "when" as well.
e.g. *bpeel kñom dtəu psaa...* = When I go to the store...
nəu bpeel kñom nəu pdtɛah, kñom aan siaw-pəu. =
When I am at home, I read books.

The word *jia-muay* means "with." It is used just like in English.
e.g. kñom dtəu saa-laa jia-muay goat. =
I go to school with him.
When you add the word *knia* to the end of *jia-muay,* this means "together."
e.g. bpuak-gee dtəu saa-laa jia-muay knia. =
They go to school together.

Tenses

Students of the Cambodian language are usually very excited to learn that Cambodian has no complicated verb conjugation based on tenses. In fact, most tenses are identified by context or by other identifying words, not by language conjugation. However, Cambodian still has three specific words to identify tenses where the tense cannot be recognized through context. These words are used before the verb to indicate the tense.

The word *baan* identifies the past tense. It is very rarely used in speech.
   e.g. kñom baan dtəʉ srok kmae. = I went to Cambodia.

baan is more commonly used in another way when describing the past tense in combination with statements involving numbers. In this circumstance, *baan* is placed before the number.
   e.g. kñom rian pia-saa kmae baan bpii chnam. =
        I have studied Cambodian for two years.

The most common way to represent the past tense is to insert another word into the sentence that indirectly identifies the tense. Cambodian people understand this much more easily.
   e.g. kñom dtəʉ srok kmae haʉy. =
        "I've already been to Cambodia." or more figuratively
        "I've been to Cambodia." or "I went to Cambodia."

The word *gɔm-bpung* identifies the present tense but only the immediate present tense. In other words, use it only to identify the tense for something that is happening at that very moment. Unlike the tense identifiers for the past and future, this identifier is used very commonly in colloquial speech.
   e.g. dtaʉ bɔɔng gɔm-bpung tvwəə ey? =
        What are you doing right now?
        kñom gɔm-bpung aan siaw-pəʉ. =
        I'm reading a book.

The word *nəng* denotes the present tense, but it is also rarely used in common speech. However, do not confuse this with other forms of the word *nəng* which are used very frequently. *nəng* is used the same way as *baan*.
   e.g. kñom nəng dtəʉ psaa. = I will go to the market.

As shown earlier, it is more common and more easily understood to use other words in the sentence that indirectly identify the tense.

kñom dtəu psaa maong-bpram-bpəl lngiak. =
I am going to the store at 7:00 p.m.

<u>Conversation 1</u>

Robert: bprək nih bɔɔng dtəɥ naa klah?
រ៉ូបឺត   ព្រឹក នេះ បង ទៅ ណា ខ្លះ
                Where are you going this morning?

Sopheap: prək nih kñom dəɥ saa-laa haɥy dtəɥ psaa dae.
សុភាព   ព្រឹក នេះ ខ្ញុំ ទៅ សាលា ហើយ ទៅ ផ្សារ ដែរ
                This morning I'm going to school and the market.

Robert: dtəɥ psaa maong bpon-maan?
រ៉ូបឺត   ទៅ ផ្សារ ម៉ោង ប៉ុន្មាន
                What time are you going to the market?

Sopheap   kñom dtəɥ maong bey. bɔɔng jɔng dtəɥ jia-muay
                kñom dtee?

សុភាព   ខ្ញុំ ទៅ ម៉ោង បី បង ចង់ ទៅ ជាមួយ
                ខ្ញុំ ទេ
                I'm going at three o'clock. Do you want to go
                with me?

Robert: baat, kñom jɔng dtəɥ. kñom soom dtəɥ baan
                dtee?

រ៉ូបឺត   បាទ ខ្ញុំ ចង់ ទៅ ខ្ញុំ សូម ទៅ បាន
                ទេ
                Yes, I do want to go. May I come?

Sopheap   baan. min-ey-dtee. juab kñom nəɥ saa-laa nəɥ
                maong bpii gɔn-lah haɥy yəəng nəng dtəɥ
                jia-muay knia.

សុភាព   បាន មិនអីទេ ជួប ខ្ញុំ នៅ សាលា នៅ
                ម៉ោង ពីរ កន្លះ ហើយ យើង នឹង ទៅ
                ជាមួយ គ្នា
                Yes, no problem. Meet me at school at 2:30, and
                we'll go together.

Conversation 2

Neang: dtau look gɔm-bpung tvwəə ey?

នាង   តើ លោក កំពុង ធ្វើ អី

What are you doing?

Rick: kñom gɔm-bpung rian pia-saa kmae. kñom rian bpii maong hauy.

វិក   ខ្ញុំ កំពុង រៀន ភាសា ខ្មែរ ខ្ញុំ រៀន

ពីរ ម៉ោង ហើយ

I am studying Cambodian. I have been studying for two hours already.

Neang: dtau pia-saa kmae bpi-baak rian dtee?

នាង   តើ ភាសា ខ្មែរ ពិបាក រៀន ទេ

Is Cambodian difficult to learn?

Rick: baat, bpi-baak nah. soom juay kñom baan dtee?

វិក   បាទ ពិបាក ណាស់ សូម ជួយ ខ្ញុំ បាន ទេ

Yes, it is very difficult. Could you please help me?

Neang: juay look baan, bpon-dtae kñom dtau juab bpuak-maak nau maong bpram.

នាង   ជួយ លោក បាន ប៉ុន្តែ ខ្ញុំ ទៅ ជួប

ពួកម៉ាក នៅ ម៉ោង ប្រាំ

Sure, I can help, but I'm going to meet a friend at five o'clock.

klia ឃ្លា **Sentences**

1. A: dtau bɔɔng jool-jet rian nəu bpeel naa?
   តើ បង ចូលចិត្ត រៀន នៅ ពេល ណា
   What time of day do you like to study?

   B: kñom jool-jet rian nəu bpeel bprək.
   ខ្ញុំ ចូលចិត្ត រៀន នៅ ពេល ព្រឹក
   I like to study in the morning.

   C: kñom jool-jẹt rian nəu bpeel yub.
   ខ្ញុំ ចូលចិត្ត រៀន នៅ ពេល យប់
   I like to study at night.

   D: kñom jool-jet rian nəu bpeel lngiak.
   ខ្ញុំ ចូលចិត្ត រៀន នៅ ពេល ល្ងាច
   I like to study in the evening.

2. A: saa-laa jab-pdtaum maong bpon-maan?
   សាលា ចាប់ផ្ដើម ម៉ោង ប៉ុន្មាន
   What time does school start?

   B: saa-laa jab-pdtaum maong-bpram-bey bprək.
   សាលា ចាប់ផ្ដើម ម៉ោង ប្រាំបី ព្រឹក
   School starts at 8:00 in the morning.

   C: saa-laa jab-pdtaum maong-bpram-bpəl gɔn-lah.
   សាលា ចាប់ផ្ដើម ម៉ោង ប្រាំពីរ កន្លះ
   School starts at 7:30.

3. A: saa-laa jɔb maong bpon-maan?
   សាលា ចប់ ម៉ោង ប៉ុន្មាន
   What time is school over?

   B: saa-laa jɔb maong-bey rosial.
   សាលា ចប់ ម៉ោង បី រសៀល
   School is over at 3:00 in the afternoon.

C: saa-laa jɔb maong-bpii-sae-seb-bpram nia-dtii.
សាលា ចប់ ម៉ោង ពីរ សែសិបប្រាំ នាទី
School is over at 2:45.

4. A: dtau bɔɔng mook dɔl bpii ɔng-gaal?
តើ បង មក ដល់ ពី អង្កាល
When did you get here?

B: kñom mook dɔl bpii maong-bpram.
ខ្ញុំ មក ដល់ ពី ម៉ោងប្រាំ
I've been here since five o'clock.

C: kñom mook dɔl dtang bpii maong-buan pluu.
ខ្ញុំ មក ដល់ តាំង ពី ម៉ោងបួន ភ្លឺ
I've been here since 4:00 am.

5. A: dtau bɔɔng jɔng dtəu pnom-bpeeñ ɔng-gaal?
តើ បង ចង់ ទៅ ភ្នំពេញ អង្កាល
When do you want to go to Phnom Penh.

B: kñom jɔng dtəu chnam nih.
ខ្ញុំ ចង់ ទៅ ឆ្នាំ នេះ
I want to go this year.

6. A: dtau look nəu psaa bpon-maan maong hauy.
តើ លោក នៅ ផ្សារ ប៉ុន្មាន ម៉ោង ហើយ
How many hours have you been at the market?

B: kñom nəu psaa bpii maong hauy.
ខ្ញុំ នៅ ផ្សារ ពីរ ម៉ោង ហើយ
I have been at the market for two hours.

C: kñom nəu psaa gɔn-lah maong hauy.
ខ្ញុំ នៅ ផ្សារ កន្លះ ម៉ោង ហើយ
I have been at the market for half an hour.

D: kñom nəu psaa dɔb nia-dtii hauy.
ខ្ញុំ នៅ ផ្សារ ដប់ នាទី ហើយ
I have been at the market for ten minutes.

7.   A: dtaɨ look jɔng tvwəə-gaa bpon-maan maong dtiat?
           តើ លោក ចង់ ធ្វើការ ប៉ុន្មាន ម៉ោង ទៀត
           How much longer do you want to work?

        B: kñom jɔng tvwəə-gaa bpii maong dtiat.
           ខ្ញុំ ចង់ ធ្វើការ ពីរ ម៉ោង ទៀត
           I want to work for two more hours.

        C: kñom jɔng tvwee-gaa muay maong gɔn-lah dtiat.
           ខ្ញុំ ចង់ ធ្វើការ មួយ ម៉ោង កន្លះ ទៀត
           I want to work for another hour and a half.

        D: kñom jɔng tvwəə-gaa dɔb-bpram nia-dtii dtiat.
           ខ្ញុំ ចង់ ធ្វើការ ដប់ប្រាំ នាទី ទៀត
           I want to work for fifteen more minutes.

        E: kñom min jɔng tvwəə-gaa dtiat dtee.
           ខ្ញុំ មិន ចង់ ធ្វើការ ទៀត ទេ
           I don't want to work any longer.

8.   A. dtaɨ bɔɔng jɔng dtəɨ srok kmae jia-muay nek naa?
           តើ បង ចង់ ទៅ ស្រុក ខ្មែរ ជាមួយ អ្នក ណា
           Who do you want to go to Cambodia with?

        B: kñom jɔng dtəɨ srok kmae jia-muay bpuak-maak.
           ខ្ញុំ ចង់ ទៅ ស្រុក ខ្មែរ ជាមួយ ពួកម៉ាក
           I want to go to Cambodia with friends.

        C: kñom jɔng dtəɨ srok kmae jia-muay grua-saa.
           ខ្ញុំ ចង់ ទៅ ស្រុក ខ្មែរ ជាមួយ គ្រួសារ
           I want to go to Cambodia with family.

        D: kñom min jɔng dtəɨ srok kmae jia-muay grua-saa
           kñom dtee.
           ខ្ញុំ មិន ចង់ ទៅ ស្រុក ខ្មែរ ជាមួយ គ្រួសារ
           ខ្ញុំ ទេ
           I don't want to go to Cambodia with my family.

Drills

1. Practice saying the following sentences in Cambodian. Some sentences can be said in different ways. If the sentence is a question, practice answering it too.

When did you get here?

_____

When are you going to Cambodia?

_____

Class starts at 7:00 in the morning.

_____

I am going to play sports with my friends.

_____

2. Do one of the following.

Create a two person dialogue about a certain activity and what time it will take place. The dialogue must have at least two parts for each participant.

Notice where you are right now. Tell yourself or someone else in Cambodian how long you have been at that place. Tell them in two different ways.

3. Use the following words to help form ten sentences.

jɔb	mi̇uay	jab-pdtaʉm
maong	saa-laa	bpon-maan
bpram	kñom	haʉy
dtang-bpii	ɔng-gaal	nih
nəʉ	bpeel	jool-jet
tvwəə-gaa	bprək	lngiak
haʉy	gɔn-lah	nia-dtii
mpei	dtəʉ	sae-seb
jɔng	jia-muay	ro-sial
buan	knia	mook
dtee	yub	dɔl

Test 5

Write these times in Cambodian.

1. 4:00 am _____

2. 6:00 pm _____

3. 12:00 am _____

4. 3:50 pm _____

5. 11:30 am _____

6. 10:45 pm _____

7. 5:05 pm _____

Write these times in English. Each time may or may not specify am or pm.

1. maong-bpram-bpəl lngiak _____

2. maong-bey plɯɯ _____

3. maong-bpram-muay-gɔn-lah bprək _____

4. maong-bpii ro-sial sae-seb-bpram nia-dtii _____

5. maong-dɔb-muay mpei-bpram nia-dtii _____

6. tngai-dtrɔng _____

7. maong-buan ro-sial _____

Translate the following into English or Cambodian.

1. kñom nəɨ pdtɛah dtang bpii maong-bey.

   ខ្ញុំ នៅ ផ្ទះ តាំង ពី ម៉ោងបី

   _____

2. ɡoat dtəɨ tvwəə-ɡaa maong-bpram bprək.

   គាត់ ទៅ ធ្វើការ ម៉ោងប្រាំ ព្រឹក

   _____

3. so-paa jool-jet ɡeeng bpeel-bprək.

   សុផា ចូលចិត្ត គេង ពេលព្រឹក

   _____

4. Tom's class ends at 4:00 pm.

   _____

5. Jenny is reading a book right now.

   _____

6. Do you want to go to the movie theater together?

   _____

Independent Vowels

Cambodian has eleven more vowel symbols which are called independent vowels. These vowels differ from the other vowels because they stand alone and do not require an accompanying consonant. Some of these vowel symbols recreate the sounds of other vowels while others have their own unique sound. Since these vowels do not interact with consonants, the /ɔɔ/ and /oo/ consonant rules do not apply to these vowels. Also, many of these sounds are so similar that it is difficult if not impossible to distinguish the differences with the transliteration system. Independent vowels are not very common, but there are many common Cambodian words which use them.

Vowel	Vowel Name	Sound
ឥ	sra-ei	/ei/
ឦ	sra-ee	/ee/
ឧ	sra-oo	/oo/
ឩ	sra-ow	/ow/
ឫ	sra-rə	/rə/
ឬ	sra-rɯɯ	/rɯɯ/

្រើ   sra-lə   /lə/

ើ   sra-luu   /luu/

ែ   sra-ae   /ae/

ៃ   sra-ai   /ai/

ៅ   sra-ao   /ao/

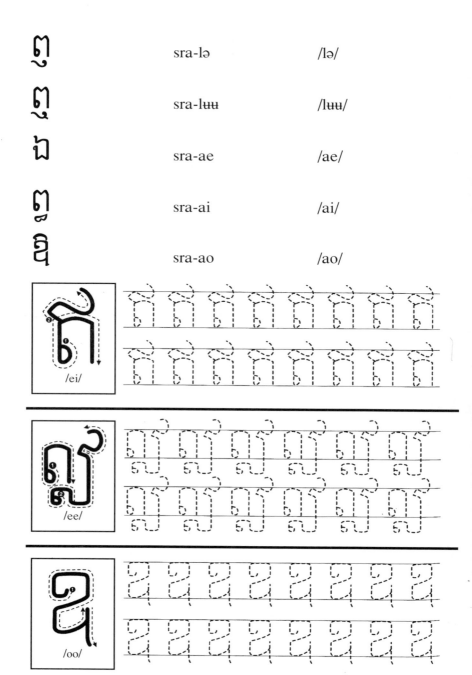

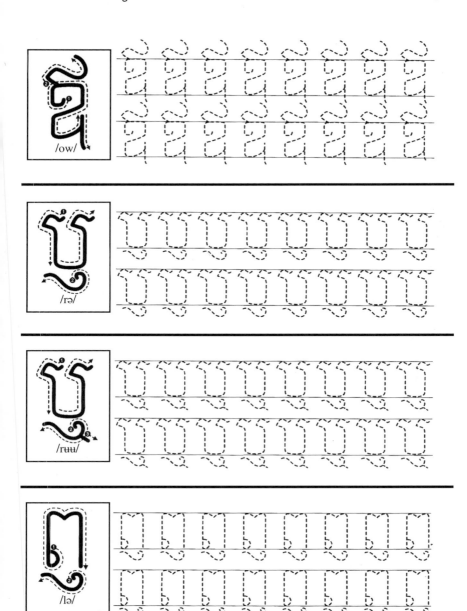

/ow/

/rə/

/rɨɨ/

/lə/

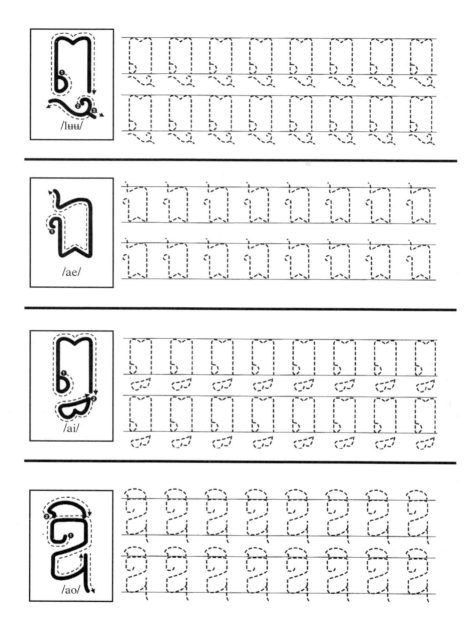

Reading Exercise: Read the following words with independent vowels, and practice writing them in Cambodian.

1. ឯ to be located at

2. ឥឡូវ right now

3. ឪពុក father

4. ឱន to bow

5. រំឭក to remind

6. ឮ to listen, hear

7. ឬ or

8. ឫស root

9. ឯង oneself

10. ឱប to hug

Sub-Consonants

We will now introduce you to a brand new part of the Cambodian alphabet: sub-consonants or *jəəng* script. Almost every consonant has a sub-consonant, i.e. lowercase, counterpart. These sub-consonants are always used after a normal uppercase consonant to form a double consonant sound. A sub-consonant can be placed in front of, below, or in back of a consonant, but the sub-consonant always gives the second part of the double consonant sound no matter where it is placed. For this reason, students can sometimes think that they are reading in circles. Nevertheless, this system is very easy to learn once you get the hang of it.

It is also important to note that all sub-consonants are of the same consonant class as their parent uppercase character. Also, the vowel sound attached to the double consonant combination generally follows the consonant class of the lowercase character because its sound comes last. However, there are exceptions which will be noted in Chapter 7.

Sub-Consonants ជើង jəəng

These are ten sub-consonants in the Cambodian alphabet. The dash represents an absent uppercase consonant.

Consonant	Pronunciation	Sound
ក	gɔɔ	/g/
ខ	kɔɔ	/k/
គ	goo	/g/
ឃ	jɔɔ	/j/
ង	joo	/j/
ច	dɔɔ/dtɔɔ	/d/, /dt/
ឆ	tɔɔ	/t/

Practice Writing Lowercase Consonants

Use ញ /-/ as the consonant when practicing the following lowercase consonants.

gaa-bpon-yul ការពន្យល់ **Explanation**

The following words are examples of double-consonant sounds in written Cambodian that involve lowercase consonants. The character-by-character explanation is presented in the order of the sounds made, not in the order of the written characters. Dashes represent absent consonants.

1. ស្គូម (sgoom) = ស + ្គ + ម
$$(s + goo + m)$$

2. ល្ខោន (lkaon) = ល + ្ខ + ោ + ន
$$(l + k + ao + n)$$

3. ម្ជុល (mjul) = ម + ្ជ + ុ + ល
$$(m + j + u + l)$$

4. ស្ដាំ (sdtam) = ស + ្ដ + ាំ
$$(s + dt + am)$$

5. ស្គរ (sgɔɔ) = ស + ្គ + រ
$$(s + gɔɔ + r) \text{ } 1$$

Note: 1. Don't forget that final *roo* (រ) consonants are silent.

Reading Exercise: Read the following words with sub-consonants, and practice writing them in Cambodian.

1. ផ្កា   flower   2. ស្ថាន   place

3. បង្ខំ   to force, compel   4. ផ្គរ   thunder

5. ស្តី   to speak   6. ផ្កាយ   star

7. ក្តាម   crab   8. ចិញ្ចឹម   to care for

Writing Exercise 5

Transcribe the following into Cambodian script using sub-consonants. These are all double consonant sounds but not all are real words. Some words can be spelled different ways. Do not use independent vowels in this exercise.

1. pgaa   _____   6. mdaay   _____

2. pdtet   _____   7. mjah   _____

3. pgoo   _____   8. lkaon   _____

4. gjɔh   _____   9. staa   _____

5. gdaam   _____   10. sjia   _____

Lesson 6

Months; days of the week; in order to;
more sub-consonants

mee-rian dtii bpram-muay មេរៀន ទី៦ Lesson 6

veak-a-sab វាក្យសព្ទ Vocabulary

tngai	ថ្ងៃ	day
aa-dtit/sa-bdaa	អាទិត្យ/សប្ដាហ៍	week[1]
kae	ខែ	month
chnam	ឆ្នាំ	year
tngai-jan	ថ្ងៃច័ន្ទ	Monday
tngai-ɔng-gia	ថ្ងៃអង្គារ	Tuesday
tngai-bput	ថ្ងៃពុធ	Wednesday
tngai-bpra-hoa	ថ្ងៃព្រហស្បតិ៍	Thursday
tngai-sok	ថ្ងៃសុក្រ	Friday
tngai-sau	ថ្ងៃសៅរ៍	Saturday
tngai-aa-dtit	ថ្ងៃអាទិត្យ	Sunday
tngai-nih	ថ្ងៃនេះ	today
sɔm-raak	សម្រាក	to rest
tngai sɔm-raak	ថ្ងៃសម្រាក	day off; holiday
bpii tngai	ពីរថ្ងៃ	two days
bey tngai	បីថ្ងៃ	three days
tngai naa	ថ្ងៃណា	which day
graoy	ក្រោយ	after, later
mun	មុន	before
gɔn-lɔɔng	កន្លង	past, already occured
aa-dtit-graoy	អាទិត្យក្រោយ	next week
aa-dtit-mun/aa-dtit gɔn-lɔɔng dtəu អាទិត្យមុន / អាទិត្យកន្លងទៅ		last week
kae-graoy	ខែក្រោយ	next month
kae-mun/kae-gɔn-lɔɔng dtəu ខែមុន / ខែកន្លងទៅ		last month
tngai-graoy	ថ្ងៃក្រោយ	a later day

sa-aek/tngai-sa-aek	ស្អែក/ថ្ងៃស្អែក	tomorrow
kaan-sa-aek	ខានស្អែក	day after tomorrow
msel-miñ	ម្សិលមិញ	yesterday
msel-mngai	ម្សិលម្ងៃ	day before yesterday
kae-mɛah-ga-raa/kae-muay ខែមករា / ខែមួយ		January[2]
kae-gom-peah/kae-bpii ខែកុម្ភៈ / ខែពីរ		February
kae-mi-nia/kae-bey ខែមិនា / ខែបី		March
kae-mee-saa/kae-buan ខែមេសា / ខែបួន		April
kae-oo-sa-pia/kae-bpram ខែឧសភា / ខែប្រាំ		May
kae-mi-to-naa/kae-bpram-muay ខែមិថុនា / ខែប្រាំមួយ		June
kae-gak-ga-daa/kae-bpram-bpəl ខែកក្កដា / ខែប្រាំពីរ		July
kae-sey-haa/kae-bpram-bey ខែសីហា / ខែប្រាំបី		August
kae-gañ-yaa/kae-bpram-buan ខែកញ្ញា / ខែប្រាំបួន		September
kae-dto-laa/kae-dɔb ខែតុលា / ខែដប់		October
kae-vwi-je-gaa/kae-dɔb-muay ខែវិច្ឆិកា / ខែដប់មួយ		November
kae-tnuu/kae-dɔb-bpii ខែធ្នូ / ខែដប់ពីរ		December
mok មុខ		ahead, front
bpii aa-dtit graoy ពីរអាទិត្យក្រោយ		two weeks from now
bey kae graoy បីខែក្រោយ		three months from now

kae-mee-saa kaang mok nih ខែមេសាខាងមុខនេះ	this coming April
kae-mun/kae-gɔn-lɔɔng-dtəɥ ខែមុន/ខែកន្លងទៅ	last month
bey-kae-mun/bey-kae-gɔn-lɔɔng-dtəɥ បីខែមុន/បីខែកន្លងទៅ	three months ago
bpii kae ពីរខែ	two months
bey kae បីខែ	three months
kae naa ខែណា	which month
daɥ-leeng ដើរលេង	to go out, recreate
dtəɥ-leeng ទៅលេង	to visit, vacation
dɔm-naɥ ដំណើរ	trip
tvwəə dɔm-naɥ ធ្វើដំណើរ	to go on a trip
git គិត	to think
tom-mdaa ធម្មតា	normal; usually
juan-gaal ជួនកាល	sometimes
daɥm-bey ដើម្បី	in order to
ro-hoot រហូត	forever, indefinitely
(ro-hoot) dɔl (រហូត) ដល់	until
jool ចូល	to enter
jeeñ ចេញ	to leave
jool geeng ចូលគេង	to go to sleep
graok-laɥng ក្រោកឡើង	to wake up

Note: 1. *sa-bdaa* is more formal than *aa-dtit*.
2. It is more common to identify a month by using the word *kae* and then adding the number of the month. The official names of months are usually used only in formal situations or broadcasts.

vwee-jia-gɔɔ   វេយ្យាករណ៍   **Grammar**

This chapter will teach you how to use the days of the week and the months of the year in Cambodian sentences. In Cambodian, the day or month usually appears at the beginning or end of a sentence. However, there is no commonly enforced grammatical rule for this.

e.g.   kae dɔb-bpii kñom dtəu-leeng grua-saa. =
I am going to visit my family in December.

e.g.   kñom jool-jet dau-leeng nəu tngai sau. =
I enjoy going out on Saturday.

When asking a question using a time identifier, always place the identifier at the end of the sentence.

e.g.   dtau bɔɔng jɔng dtəu kae naa? =
When do you want to go?

It is very simple to express a period of time with multiple days or months. *bpii* is inserted before the time indicator phrase and *dtəu, dɔl,* or *ro-hoot dɔl* is inserted between the two time identifying words in the following manner. The word *ro-hoot* gives the indication that the action performed was uninterrupted.

e.g.   kñom dtəu saa-laa bpii tngai-jan dɔl tngai-sok. =
I go to school from Monday to Friday.

e.g.   goat tvwəə-gaa bpii maong-bpram ro-hoot-dɔl maong bpii.
He works from 5:00 until 2:00.

The words *juan-gaal* or *tom-mdaa* are usuallly used at the beginning of a sentence. The time indicator word then comes at the end.

e.g.   tom-mdaa kñom ñam baay nəu bpeel-lngiak. =
I usually eat in the evening.

As you may have already noticed, the word *leeng* can be combined with other verbs. Since *leeng* means "to play," this indicates a playful and pleasant nature to the verb. Oftentimes, there is no object when this type of verb is used. The following are some examples.

e.g.   *aan-leeng* - This means to read for enjoyment. Studying a book for a test would not be the proper situation to use this word, but reading a newspaper or novel would be.

e.g.   *dtəu-leeng* - This means to go somewhere for pleasure. In other words, a vacation. Something like a business trip would not qualify as proper usage of this word.

<u>Conversation</u>

Sue: chnam nih kñom jɔng dtəʉ srok-kmae.
ស៊ូ   ឆ្នាំ នេះ ខ្ញុំ ចង់ ទៅ ស្រុកខ្មែរ
     I would like to go to Cambodia this year.

Sophal: jɔng dtəʉ srok-kmae tvwəə ey?
សុផល   ចង់ ទៅ ស្រុកខ្មែរ ធ្វើ អី
     What do you want to do in Cambodia?

Sue: kñom jɔng dtəʉ daʉm-bey tvwəə-gaa.
ស៊ូ   ខ្ញុំ ចង់ ទៅ ដើម្បី ធ្វើការ
     I want to go in order to work (there).

Sophal: dtaʉ bɔɔng jɔng dtəʉ ɔng-gaal?
សុផល   តើ បង ចង់ ទៅ អង្កាល
     When do you want to go?

Sue: kñom git taa dtəʉ kae-bpram.
ស៊ូ   ខ្ញុំ គិត ថា ទៅ ខែប្រាំ
     I think that I want to go in May.

Sophal: haʉy jɔng nəʉ bpon-maan kae?
សុផល   ហើយ ចង់ នៅ ប៉ុន្មាន ខែ
     And how many weeks do you want to stay there?

Sue: kñom jɔng nəʉ bey kae, bpii kae-bpram
     ro-hoot dɔl kae-bpram-bpəl.
ស៊ូ   ខ្ញុំ ចង់ នៅ បី ខែ ពី ខែប្រាំ
     រហូត ដល់ ខែប្រាំពីរ
     I would like to go for three months, from May to July.

Sophal: baʉ bɔɔng dtəʉ meeñ, kñom gɔɔ jɔng dtəʉ dae.
សុផល   បើ បង ទៅ មែន ខ្ញុំ ក៏ ចង់ ទៅ ដែរ
     If you're really going, I want to go too.

klia   ឃ្លា   **Sentences**

1.   A: tngai-nih jɔng tvwəə ey?
           ថ្ងៃនេះ   ចង់   ធ្វើ   អី
           What do you want to do today?

        B: tngai-nih kñom jɔng daʉ-leeng.
           ថ្ងៃនេះ   ខ្ញុំ   ចង់   ដើរលេង
           I would like to go out today.

2.   A: msel-miñ bɔɔng daʉ-leeng nəʉ ae naa?
           ម្សិលមិញ   បង   ដើរលេង   នៅ ឯ ណា
           Where did you go yesterday?

        B: msel-miñ kñom daʉ-leeng nəʉ bat-dɔm-bɔɔng.
           ម្សិលមិញ   ខ្ញុំ   ដើរលេង   នៅ   បាត់ដំបង
           Yesterday, I went to visit Battambang.

3.   A: sa-aek look jɔng dtəʉ-leeng nek naa klah?
           ស្អែក   លោក ចង់   ទៅ លេង អ្នក ណា ខ្លះ
           Who would you like to visit tomorrow?

        B: sa-aek kñom jɔng dtəʉ-leeng grua-saa nəng
           bpuak-maak.
           ស្អែក   ខ្ញុំ   ចង់   ទៅលេង   គ្រួសារ   និង
           ពួកម៉ាក
           Tomorrow I want to visit family and friends.

4.   A: dtaʉ bɔɔng dtiñ pdtɛah bpii ɔng-gaal?
           តើ   បង   ទិញ   ផ្ទះ   ពី   អង្កាល
           When did you buy a home?

        B: kñom dtiñ pdtɛah dtang-bpii kae dɔb.
           ខ្ញុំ   ទិញ   ផ្ទះ   តាំងពី   ខែ   ដប់
           I bought a home in October.

        C: kñom dtiñ pdtɛah bey kae haʉy.
           ខ្ញុំ   ទិញ   ផ្ទះ   បី   ខែ   ហើយ
           Three months ago, I bought a house.

5. A: dtau booong jong dtiñ laan oong-gaal?
    តើ បង ចង់ ទិញ ឡាន អង្កាល
    When do you want to buy a car?

    B: kñom dtiñ laan kae-graoy.
    ខ្ញុំ ទិញ ឡាន ខែក្រោយ
    I will buy a car next month.

    C: kñom nəng dtiñ laan kae-dɔb-muay kaang-mok-nih .
    ខ្ញុំ នឹង ទិញ ឡាន ខែដប់មួយ ខាងមុខនេះ
    I will buy a car this coming November.

    D: bpii aa-dtit dtiat, kñom nəng dtiñ laan.
    ពីរ អាទិត្យ ទៀត ខ្ញុំ នឹង ទិញ ឡាន
    I will buy a car in two weeks.

6. A: dtau booong jong sɔm-raak nəu tngai naa?
    តើ បង ចង់ សម្រាក នៅ ថ្ងៃ ណា
    What day do you want to rest?

    B: kñom jong sɔm-raak nəu tngai sau.
    ខ្ញុំ ចង់ សម្រាក នៅ ថ្ងៃ សៅរ៍
    I want to rest on Saturday.

7. A: dtau look tvwəə-gaa nəu tngai naa klah?
    តើ លោក ធ្វើការ នៅ ថ្ងៃ ណា ខ្លះ
    What days do you work?

    B: kñom tvwəə-gaa bpii tngai-ɔng-gia dtəu tngai-sau.
    ខ្ញុំ ធ្វើការ ពី ថ្ងៃអង្គារ ទៅ ថ្ងៃសៅរ៍
    I work from Tuesday to Saturday.

8.   kñom nəu saa-laa bpii maong-bpram-bey dɔl
        maong-bpii.
        ខ្ញុំ នៅ សាលា ពី ម៉ោងប្រាំបី ដល់
        ម៉ោងពីរ
        I am at school from 8:00 until 2:00.

9. A: tom-mdaa, look jool geeng maong bpon-mann?
    ធម្មតា លោក ចូល គេង ម៉ោង ប៉ុន្មាន
    When do you usually go to sleep?

B: tom-mdaa kñom jool geeng maong-dɔb-muay.

ធម្មតា ខ្ញុំ ចូល គេង ម៉ោងដប់មួយ

I usually go to bed at 11:00.

10.   A: juan-gaal bɔɔng jool-jet tvwəə a-vwey klah?

ជួនកាល បង ចូលចិត្ត ធ្វើ អ្វី ខ្លះ

What do you occasionally like to do?

B: juan-gaal, kñom jool-jet məəl dtuu-rə-dtuah.

ជួនកាល ខ្ញុំ ចូលចិត្ត មើល ទូរទស្សន៍

Occasionally, I like to watch television.

11.   tom-mdaa, kñom nəu bprɔ-dteeh-jo-bpun bpii
kae-gom-bpeah ro-hoot dɔl kae-mee-saa.

ធម្មតា ខ្ញុំ នៅ ប្រទេសជប៉ុន ពី
ខែកុម្ភៈ រហូត ដល់ ខែមេសា

I am usually in Japan from February until April.

12.   kñom tvwəə-gaa daum-bey luy.

ខ្ញុំ ធ្វើការ ដើម្បី លុយ

I work in order to have money.

13.   goat rian pia-saa kmae daum-bey juab bpuak-maak
kmae.

គាត់ រៀន ភាសា ខ្មែរ ដើម្បី ជួប ពួកម៉ាក
ខ្មែរ

She studies Cambodian in order to meet Cambodian
friends.

Drills

1. Practice saying the following sentences in Cambodian. Some sentences can be said in different ways. If the sentence is a question, practice answering it too.

Yesterday, I went to the movie theater.

I go to Cambodia in order to study the Cambodian language.

I usually read the newspaper in the morning.

When did you go to Phnom Penh?

When were you in France?

2. Do the following.

Create a two person dialogue about a trip you are planning. Include when you are leaving and the length of time that you will be gone in months.

Compose a paragraph telling when you usually go to sleep, how long you sleep and when you usually wake up.

3. Use the following words to help form ten sentences.

bɔɔng	tngai-sok	daʉm-bey
ro-hoot dɔl	bpii	rian
daʉ-leeng	dtəʉ-leeng	kae-mun
tngai-jan	kae-muay	msel-mngai
kñom	kae-bpram	baan
goat	gɔn-lɔɔng-dtəʉ	juab
kae	mok	dtəʉ
nəʉ	tvwəə	juan-gaal
dɔm-naʉ	jɔng	tom-mdaa
bpram	maong	saa-laa
kae-graoy	buan	aa-dtit
srok kmae	tvwəə-gaa	srok jen
jool	jeeñ	geeng

Test 6

Match the following days and months with the appropriate Cambodian word.

Months

_____ 1. January   a. kae-mee-saa ខែមេសា

_____ 2. February   b. kae-dto-laa ខែតុលា

_____ 3. March   c. kae-gak-ga-daa ខែកក្កដា

_____ 4. April   d. kae-gom-bpeah ខែកុម្ភៈ

_____ 5. May   e. kae-oo-sa-pia ខែឧសភា

_____ 6. June   f. kae-sey-haa ខែសីហា

_____ 7. July   g. kae-tnuu ខែធ្នូ

_____ 8. August   h. kae-mɛah-ga-raa មករា

_____ 9. September   i. kae-mi-to-naa ខែមិថុនា

_____ 10. October   j. kae-vwi-je-gaa ខែវិច្ឆិកា

_____ 11. November   k. kae-gañ-yaa ខែកញ្ញា

_____ 12. December   l. kae-mii-nia ខែមីនា

Days

_____ 1. Monday   a. tngai-bput ថ្ងៃពុធ

_____ 2. Tuesday   b. tngai-sok ថ្ងៃសុក្រ

_____ 3. Wednesday   c. tngai-jan ថ្ងៃចន្ទ

_____ 4. Thursday   d. tngai-aa-dtit ថ្ងៃអាទិត្យ

_____ 5. Friday   e tngai-sau ថ្ងៃសៅរ៍

_____ 6. Saturday   f. tngai-ɔng-gia ថ្ងៃអង្គារ

_____ 7. Sunday   g. tngai-bpra-hoa ថ្ងៃព្រហស្បតិ៍

Translate the following into English or Cambodian.

1. kñom sɔm-raak bpii tngai-sau dɔl tngai jan.

    ខ្ញុំ   សម្រាក   ពី   ថ្ងៃសៅរ៍   ដល់   ថ្ងៃចន្ទ

    _____

2. juan-gaal, kñom jool geeng maong dɔb-bpii.

    ជួនកាល   ខ្ញុំ   ចូល   គេង   ម៉ោងដប់ពីរ

    _____

3. goat dtəu psaa daum-bey dtiñ siaw-pəu.

    គាត់   ទៅ   ផ្សារ   ដើម្បី   ទិញ   សៀវភៅ

    _____

4. In two weeks, I am going to Vietnam.

    _____

5. He has been here since 6:00.

    _____

Sub-Consonants ເຜີຖ jəəng

These are six more sub-consonants in the Cambodian alphabet. The dash represents an absent uppercase consonant.

Consonant	Pronunciation	Sound
ញ	dtoo	/dt/
្ប	bɔɔ	/b/
្ត	bpoo	/bp/
្ប	poo	/p/
្ស	sɔɔ	/s/
្ហ	hɔɔ	/h/
្អ	ɔɔ	/ɔ/

Practice Writing Lowercase Consonants

Use ញ /-/ as the consonant when practicing the following lowercase consonants.

gaa-bpon-yul ការពន្យល់ **Explanation**

When the /ɔɔ/ (្) sub-consonant modifies the *initial* consonant in a word, it produces another syllable after the consonant it modifies.

e.g. ផ្អែម (pa-aem) = ផ + ្ + េ- + ម

$$(p + a + ae + m)$$

ស្អាត (sa-aat) = ស + ្ + -ា + ត

$$(s + a + aa + t)$$

Reading Exercise: Read the following words with sub-consonants, and practice writing them in Cambodian.

1. ស្ទឹង small river

2. ឆ្អែត full, satisfied

3. ក្បាល head

4. ស្ពាន bridge

5. ស្ទាប to touch

6. ផ្សេង different

7. បង្ហាញ to show, reveal

8. ស្អាត pretty, clean

9. ខ្សែ string

10. ល្ហុង papaya

11. ម្ភៃ twenty

12. ដើម្បី in order to

Read and translate the following sentences.

1. បង បាន ទៅ រាងកុន

2. ខ្ញុំ សូម អាន សៀវភៅ បាន ទេ

3. តើ លោក មក ពី ណា

4. ផ្សារ នៅ ជិត នេះ

5. លោក រៀន នៅ ណា ដែរ

Writing Exercise 6

Transcribe the following into Cambodian script. These are all real Cambodian words. However, you may be able to phonetically spell them in several different ways.

1. psaeng _____   6. dtboong _____

2. sbpək _____   7. pa-aul _____

3. sdtuuik _____   8. mhoob _____

4. jbaa _____   9. msau _____

5. sa-ey _____   10. sdteah _____

Lesson 7

Telephone conversations; *tloab* and *dael*; food;
more sub-consonants

mee-rian dtii bpram-bpii មេរៀន ទី៧ **Lesson 7**

vɛak-a-sab វាក្យសព្ទ **Vocabulary**

bpraн	ប្រើ	to use
haet a-vwey	ហេតុអ្វី	why
som	សុំ	to ask (for something)
gɔɔ-baan	ក៏បាន	okay, all right
bpii-bpruah/bpruah	ពីព្រោះ / ព្រោះ	because
sɔm-rab	សំរាប់	for
min sɔнw	មិនសូវ	not so...
tloab/dael	ធ្លាប់ / ដែល	to have ever done something, to experience
aa-loo/jɔm-riab-sua	អាឡូ / ជំរាបសួរ	hello (on the phone)
juab knia tngai graoy (dtiat) ជួបគ្នាថ្ងៃក្រោយ(ទៀត)		"I'll see you later."
jam	ចាំ	to remember; to wait[1]
muay-plɛɛt	មួយភ្លែត	one moment
soom jam muay-plɛɛt	សូមចាំមួយភ្លែត	"One moment please."
jih	ជិះ	to ride
sii-kloo	ស៊ីក្លូ	pedicab
moo-dtoo	ម៉ូតូ	motorcycle
mhoob	ម្ហូប	food[2]
mhoob kmae	ម្ហូបខ្មែរ	Cambodian food
mhoob aa-mee-ri-gang	ម្ហូបអាមេរិកាំង	American food
mhoob tai	ម្ហូបថៃ	Thai food
mhoob baa-rang	ម្ហូបបារាំង	French food
tvwəə baay/tvwəə mhoob	ធ្វើបាយ/ធ្វើម្ហូប	to cook
jet	ចិត	to peel, slice

bong-aem បង្អែម	dessert
jong-graan-baay ចង្រ្កានបាយ	kitchen
klian (baay) / heew (baay) ឃ្លាន (បាយ) / ហេវ (បាយ)	hungry
cha-aet ឆ្អែត	full
chngañ ឆ្ងាញ់	tasty, delicious
min chngañ/ot chngañ មិនឆ្ងាញ់ / អត់ឆ្ងាញ់	not tasty
pa-aem ផ្អែម	sweet
juu ជូរ	sour
bprai ប្រៃ	salty
lvwiing/jot ល្វីង / ចត់	bitter
saab សាប	bland, tasteless
hol ហឹរ	spicy
bpeek ពេក	too...
jraɯn bpeek ច្រើនពេក	too much
bon-dtek បន្តិច	a little
bon-dtek dtiat បន្តិចទៀត	a little more
taem (dtiat) ថែម (ទៀត)	more
soom សម	fork
slaab-bpria ស្លាបព្រា	spoon
gam-bet កាំបិត	knife
jong-goh ចង្កឹះ	chopsticks
baay បាយ	rice; food
saik សាច់	meat
saik-goo សាច់គោ	beef
saik-moan សាច់មាន់	chicken
saik-jruuk សាច់ជ្រូក	pork
som-loo/sub សម្ល/ស៊ុប	soup
chaa ឆា	stir fry
baay chaa បាយឆា	fried rice
plae-choo ផ្លែឈើ	fruit

bɔn-lae	បន្លែ	vegetables
dtrey	ត្រី	fish
sot	សុទ្ធ	pure
dtək	ទឹក	water; fluid
dtək saab	ទឹកសាប	water
dtək sot/dtək bɔɔ-ri-sot	ទឹកសុទ្ធ / ទឹកបរិសុទ្ធ	purified water; bottled water
dtək maa-sin	ទឹកម៉ាស៊ីន	tap water
dtək plae-chəə	ទឹកផ្លែឈើ	fruit juice
dtək krooik	ទឹកក្រូច	orange juice, soda

Note: 1. *jam* has two different meanings, but it is pronounced exactly the same.

2. Unlike the word *baay* which can mean either cooked rice or food, *mhoob* only means food.

vwee-jia-gɔɔ   វេយ្យាករណ៍   **Grammar**

This chapter does not introduce much new grammar, but there are some new items that should be mentioned.

In Cambodian, the words *tloab* and *dael* are used to make inquiries regarding someone's experience. When responding to a question of this nature, the word *tloab* is generally used to make positive responses and the work *dael* is generally used to make negative responses.

> e.g. dtau look dael dtəu srok kmae dtee? =
> Have you ever been to Cambodia?
> baat, kñom tloab dtəu srok kmae. =
> Yes, I have been to Cambodia.
> ɔt-dtee, kñom min dael dtəu srok kmae dtee. =
> No, I have never been to Cambodia.

The phrase *min səuw* means "not very..." or "not so..." and is used in the same way it would be used in English.

> e.g. nih min səuw tlai dtee.
> This is not very expensive.

bpii-bpruah or *bpruah* means "because," and it is used the same way as it is used in English.

> e.g. haet-avwey bɔng min jɔng dtəu? =
> Why do you not want to go?
> kñom min jɔng dtəu bpii-bpruah kñom jɔng məəl gon. =
> I don't want to go because I want to watch a movie.

The word *som* is different from the word *soom* in one important aspect. *soom* is used for asking permission to do something. *som* is used when asking for something.

> e.g kñom soom dtəu ñam baay, baan dtee?
> May I please go eat?
> kñom som baay taem dtiat, baan dtee?
> May I please have some more rice?

Note on Telephone Conversations

The first dialogue in this chapter will show a typical example of a Cambodian telephone conversation. Unlike English, merely asking if a person is home does not necessarily mean that you wish to speak to that person. Generally, you must first ask if the person is home and then ask to speak with the person after you have received your answer.

A common way to ask if someone is home is as follows.
e.g. dtaʉ (name) nəʉ pdtɛah dtee? =
Is (name) at home?

This literally asks if that person is at the house. A more informal or colloquial expression is to omit the word *dtaʉ* and *pdtɛah* from the above question. This adjusted phrase asks if the person is "there," not if they are "at home."
e.g. (name) nəʉ dtee? = Is (name) there?

After you have established that a person is home, you must ask to speak with that person using the previously learned method of asking permission.
e.g. kñom soom ni-yiay jia-muay (name) baan dtee? =
May I please speak with (name)?

Perhaps the most awkward part of a phone conversation in Cambodian is the goodbye. Oftentimes, the word "goodbye" is not spoken at all. The conversation is simply (and abruptly) cut off when both parties realize that there is nothing left to say.

Conversation 1

Sambat: aa-loo?
សម្បត្តិ   អាឡោ
   Hello?

Ron: baat, bɔɔng so-kaa nəʉ pdtɛah dtee?
រ៉ន   បាទ បង សុខា នៅ ផ្ទះ ទេ
   Yes, is Sokha home?

Sambat: baat, goat nəʉ.
សម្បត្តិ   បាទ គាត់ នៅ
   Yes, she is here.

Ron: kñom soom ni-yiay jia-muay goat baan dtee?
រ៉ន   ខ្ញុំ សូម និយាយ ជាមួយ គាត់ បាន ទេ
   May I please speak with her?

Sambat: baan, soom jam muay-plɛɛt.
សម្បត្តិ   បាន សូម ចាំ មួយភ្លែត
   Yes, please hold on a moment.

Sokha: aa-loo?
សុខា   អាឡោ
   Hello?

Ron: baat, kñom jia bɔɔng rɔɔn. dtaʉ bɔɔng
   sok-sɔb-baay dtee?
រ៉ន   បាទ ខ្ញុំ ជា បង រ៉ន តើ បង
   សុខសប្បាយ ទេ
   Yes, this is Ron. How are your doing?

Sokha: jaah, kñom sok-sɔb-baay.
សុខា   ចាំ ខ្ញុំ សុខសប្បាយ
   I'm doing fine.

Ron: yub nih, kñom haʉy-nəng bpuak-maak kñom
   jong dtəʉ ñam mhoob kmae. dtaʉ bɔɔng jong
   dtəʉ dae rʉʉ dtee?

រ៉ុន យប់ នេះ ខ្ញុំ ហើយនិង ពួកម៉ាក ខ្ញុំ
ចង់ ទៅ ញ៉ាំ មួប ខ្មែរ តើ បង ចង់
ទៅ ដែរ ឬ ទេ

Tonight my friends and I want to go eat
Cambodian food. Do you want to go too?

Sokha: jaa, kñom jɔng dtəɯ. yəəng juab knia maong
bpon-maan?

សុខា ចា៎ ខ្ញុំ ចង់ ទៅ យើង ជួប គ្នា ម៉ោង
ប៉ុន្មាន

Yes, I would like to go. What time are we going to
meet?

Ron: aaik juab nəɯ pdtɛah kñom maong bpram-muay
baan dtee?

រ៉ុន អាច ជួប នៅ ផ្ទះ ខ្ញុំ ម៉ោង ប្រាំមួយ
បាន ទេ

Can you meet at my house at 6:00?

Sokha: baan. kñom aaik juab bɔɔng nəɯ maong
bpram-muay baan.

សុខា បាន ខ្ញុំ អាច ជួប បង នៅ ម៉ោង
ប្រាំមួយ បាន

That's fine. I'll meet you at 6:00.

Ron: baat. ɔɔ-gun. jəm-riab-lia.

រ៉ុន បាទ អរគុណ ជំរាបលា

Thanks. Goodbye.

Sokha: jaa. jəm-riab-lia.

សុខា ចា៎ ជំរាបលា

Goodbye.

Conversation 2

Srey: dtaɰ look tloab ñam mhoob kmae dtee?

ស្រី   តើ លោក ធ្លាប់ ញ៉ាំ មូប ខ្មែរ ទេ

       Have you ever eaten Cambodian food?

Tom: baat, kñom tloab.

ថម   បាទ ខ្ញុំ ធ្លាប់

       Yes, I have.

Srey: dtaɰ look git taa mhoob kmae chngañ dtee?

ស្រី   តើ លោក គិត ថា មូប ខ្មែរ ឆ្ងាញ់ ទេ

       Do you think that Cambodian food tastes good?

Tom: kñom taa chngañ bpon-dtae kñom min sɔɰw

       jeh bpraɰ jong-gəh dtee.[1]

ថម   ខ្ញុំ ថា ឆ្ងាញ់ ប៉ុន្តែ ខ្ញុំ មិន សូវ

       ចេះ ប្រើ ចង្កឹះ ទេ

       I think it's tasty, but I don't know how to use

       chopsticks very well.

Srey: min-ey-dtee. look aaik bpraɰ slaab-bpria nəng

       sɔɔm gɔɔ-baan dae.

ស្រី   មិនអីទេ លោក អាច ប្រើ ស្លាបព្រា និង

       សម ក៏បាន ដែរ

       That's okay. You can use a spoon and fork.

Note: 1. In this sentence, *taa* is used without a vowel such as *git* or *dəng*
          preceding it. This is very common in colloquial Cambodian
          speech.

klia   ឃ្លា   **Sentences**

1.   A: dtau look dael məəl gon nih dtee?
         តើ លោក ដែល មើល កុន នេះ ទេ
         Have you ever seen this movie?

      B: baat, kñom tloab məəl gon nih.
         បាទ ខ្ញុំ ធ្លាប់ មើល កុន នេះ
         Yes, I have seen this movie.

      C: ɔt-dtee. kñom min dael məəl gon nih dtee.
         អត់ទេ ខ្ញុំ មិន ដែល មើល កុន នេះ ទេ
         No, I have never seen this movie.

2.   A: dtau bɔɔng tloab jih sii-kloo dtee?
         តើ បង ធ្លាប់ ជិះ ស៊ីក្លូ ទេ
         Have you ever ridden a pedicab?

      B: jaa, kñom tloab jih.
         ចា៎ ខ្ញុំ ធ្លាប់ ជិះ
         Yes, I have ridden (one).

      C: ɔt-dtee. kñom min dael jih dtee.
         អត់ទេ ខ្ញុំ មិន ដែល ជិះ ទេ
         No, I have never ridden (one).

3.   kñom tloab dtəu leeng srok tai.
         ខ្ញុំ ធ្លាប់ ទៅ លេង ស្រុក ថៃ
         I have gone on a trip to Thailand.

4.   A: mhoob kmae həl dtee?
         ម្ហូប ខ្មែរ ហឺរ ទេ
         Is Cambodian food spicy?

      B: mhoob kmae min səuw həl bpon-maan dtee.
         ម្ហូប ខ្មែរ មិន សូវ ហឺរ ប៉ុន្មាន ទេ
         Cambodian food is not very spicy.

5.   A: laan goat tom dtee?
         ឡាន គាត់ ធំ ទេ
         Is his car big?

         B: laan goat min səɯw tom bpon-maan dtee.
         ឡាន គាត់ មិន សូវ ធំ ប៉ុន្មាន ទេ
         His car is not very big.

6.   A: haet-a-vwey bɔɔng ɔt jool-jet mhoob ba-raang?
         ហេតុអ្វី បង អត់ ចូលចិត្ត ម្ហូប បារាំង
         Why don't you like French food?

         B. bpii-bpruah mhoob ba-raang saab bpeek.
         ពីព្រោះ ម្ហូប បារាំង សាប ពេក
         Because French food is too bland.

7.   A: haet-a-vwey goat ɔt mian laan.
         ហេតុអ្វី គាត់ អត់ មាន ឡាន
         Why doesn't he have a car?

         B: bpruah goat ɔt mian luy dtiñ laan dtee.
         ព្រោះ គាត់ អត់ មាន លុយ ទិញ ឡាន ទេ
         Because he doen't have money to buy a car.

8.   A: haet-a-vwey goat ɔt jool-jet tvwəə-baay?
         ហេតុអ្វី គាត់ អត់ ចូលចិត្ត ធ្វើបាយ
         Why doesn't she like to cook?

         B: goat ɔt jool-jet bpii-bpruah goat min jeh.
         គាត់ អត់ ចូលចិត្ត ពីព្រោះ គាត់ មិន ចេះ
         She doesn't like to cook because she doesn't know
         how.

9.   A: sɔm-lɔɔ nih chngañ dtee?
         សម្ល នេះ ឆ្ងាញ់ ទេ
         Does this soup taste good?

         B: baat, chngañ.
         បាទ ឆ្ងាញ់
         Yes, it tastes good.

C: ɔt-dtee, min səʉw chngañ dtee.

អត់ទេ មិន សូវ ឆ្ងាញ់ ទេ

No, it's not very tasty.

D: min chngañ dtee. sɔm-lɔɔ nih bprai bpeek.

មិន ឆ្ងាញ់ ទេ សម្ល នេះ ប្រៃ ពេក

No, it doesn't taste good. It's too salty.

10. A: jɔng taem dtiat dtee?

ចង់ ថែម ទៀត ទេ

Would you like some more?

B: baat, kñom som bɔn-dtek dtiat.

បាទ ខ្ញុំ សុំ បន្តិច ទៀត

Yes, I would like a little more.

C: min-ey-dtee kñom cha-aet haʉy. ɔɔ-gun.

មិនអីទេ ខ្ញុំ ឆ្អែត ហើយ អរគុណ

That's all right. I'm full. Thank you.

11. A: dtaʉ bɔɔng jeh ñam mhoob həl dtee?[1]

តើ បង ចេះ ញាំ ម្ហូប ហឹរ ទេ

Do you like to eat spicy food?

B: baat, kñom jeh.

បាទ ខ្ញុំ ចេះ

Yes, I like it.

C: ɔt-dtee, kñom min jeh ñam dtee.

អត់ទេ ខ្ញុំ មិន ចេះ ញាំ ទេ

No, I do not like it.

12. kñom bpraʉ gam-bet sɔm-rab jet bɔn-lae.

ខ្ញុំ ប្រើ កាំបិត សំរាប់ ចិត បន្លែ

I use a knife to slice vegetables.

13. goat jool-jet ñam plae-chəə haʉy-nəng dtək-sot.

គាត់ ចូលចិត្ត ញាំ ផ្លែឈើ ហើយនឹង ទឹកសុទ្ធ

He likes to eat fruit and drink bottled water.

14.   goat ñam baay jraʉn bpeek.

គាត់ ញ៉ាំ បាយ ច្រើន ពេក

He eats too much food.

15:    A: dtaʉ bɔɔng klian baay dtee?

តើ បង ឃ្លាន បាយ ទេ

Are you hungry?

      B: baat, kñom klian baay.

បាទ ខ្ញុំ ឃ្លាន បាយ

Yes, I am hungry.

      C: baat, kñom klian baay nah.

បាទ ខ្ញុំ ឃ្លាន បាយ ណាស់

Yes, I am very hungry.

      D: dtee, kñom min klian baay dtee.

ទេ ខ្ញុំ មិន ឃ្លាន បាយ ទេ

No, I am not hungry.

16.   A: kñom jam goat bpii maong haʉy.

ខ្ញុំ ចាំ គាត់ ពីរ ម៉ោង ហើយ

I have been waiting for him for two hours already.

      B: kñom ɔt jam goat dtee.

ខ្ញុំ អត់ ចាំ គាត់ ទេ

I don't remember him.

17.   kñom dtiñ siaw-pəʉw sɔm-rab məəl.

ខ្ញុំ ទិញ សៀវភៅ សំរាប់ មើល

I buy books for reading.

Note: 1. When asking if you like a certain food in Cambodian, you usually use the word *jeh*. In fact, you are literally asking if the person knows "how to eat the food." Many foreigners find this strange and may be confused. In Cambodian, if you know "how to" eat something, that means you like it. If you don't know "how to" eat it, that means you don't like it. Now you will know not to answer this question by saying, "Put it in your mouth, chew it, and swallow it!'

Drills

1. Practice saying the following sentences in Cambodian. If the sentence is a question, practice answering it as well.

I have too many books.

_____

What foods do you like to eat?

_____

Have you ever visited Siem Reap?

_____

Why do you use chopsticks?

_____

She drinks bottled water, but she does not drink tap water.

_____

2. Do the following.

Create a dialogue asking someone what kind of food they like. Ask that person why they like it and have the person give an answer (because it's sweet, delicious, etc.)

Compose a short telephone conversation between two people that has each of the following parts: an opening greeting, asking if the person is home, and asking the receiver of the call if he or she wants to do something with the caller.

3. Use the following words to help form ten sentences.

ɔt	mhoob	jeh
ñam	hauy	bprai
nəu	kñom	jool-jet
aa-mee-ri-gang	baay-chaa	tloab
bpii-bpruah	chngañ	jam
soom	dtee	dtəu
srok	baa-rang	yuu
bɔɔng	pa-aem	goat
həl	nah	tai
muay-plɛɛt	pdtɛah	bpeek
kmae	sɔm-lɔɔ	baay
jɔng	jia-muay	dael
goat	min	ey
klah	nəng	baan

Test 7

Match the English words with the Cambodian words.

_____ 1. bitter   a. bpeek ពោក

_____ 2. fish   b. chngañ ឆ្ងាញ់

_____ 3. sour   c. bpii-bpruah ពីព្រោះ

_____ 4. delicious   d. sɔɔm សម

_____ 5. food   e. dtrey ត្រី

_____ 6. salty   f. klian ឃ្លាន

_____ 7. beef   g. juu ជូរ

_____ 8. full   h. slaab-bpria ស្លាបព្រា

_____ 9. spoon   i. bprai ប្រៃ

_____ 10. hungry   j. saik-goo សាច់គោ

_____ 11. because   k. lvwiing ល្វីង

_____ 12. fork   l. mhoob ម្ហូប

                           m. cha-aet ឆ្អែត

Translate the following into English or Cambodian.

1. kñom jeh ñam mhoob kmae, bpon-dtae ɔt jeh ñam mhoob vwiat-naam dtee.

   ខ្ញុំ ចេះ ញ៉ាំ ម្ហូប ខ្មែរ ប៉ុន្តែ អត់ ចេះ ញ៉ាំ ម្ហូប វៀតណាម ទេ

   _____

2. bɔɔng so-kaa nəɯ pdtɛah dtee?

   បង សុខា នៅ ផ្ទះ ទេ

   _____

3. nəɯ bpeel kñom ñam mhoob kmae, kñom bpraɯ jɔng-gəh.

   នៅ ពេល ខ្ញុំ ញ៉ាំ ម្ហូប ខ្មែរ ខ្ញុំ ប្រើ ចង្កឹះ

   _____

4. This soup is too salty.

   _____

5. I have eaten French food before.

   _____

Sub-Consonants ជើង jəəng

These sub-consonants are all /oo/ class sub-consonants that do not determine the vowel sound of the word they are used with. When using only these sub-consonants, the vowel sound is determined by the class of the uppercase consonant.

Consonant	Pronunciation	Sound
ង	ngoo	/ng/
ញ	ñoo	/ñ/[1]
ញ	ñoo	/ñ/[1]
ណ	noo	/n/
ន	moo	/m/
យ	yoo	/y/
រ	roo	/r/
ល	loo	/l/
វ	vwoo	/vw/

Note: 1. There are two different lowercase consonants for ញ ñoo.

Practice Writing Lowercase Consonants

Use ញ /-/ as the consonant when practicing the following lowercase consonants.

gaa-bpon-yul ការពន្យល់ **Explanation**

Congratulations! You have now finally reached your first set of "exceptions" in the Cambodian writing system. Unlike other sub-consonants, all of the sub-consonants introduced in this chapter adopt the consonant class of the uppercase consonant to which they are attached. In other words, the consonant class of the uppercase consonant dominates the consonant class of the sub-consonant. These are the only sub-consonants in the alphabet that do not dominate the class of the uppercase consonant.

e.g. ថ (tɔɔ) + ្ល (jəəng loo) + ា (sra aa) = ថ្លា (tlaa)

Please note that even though the sub-consonant sound is pronounced after the uppercase consonant sound, the class of the uppercase consonant dominates and determines the vowel sound. The word formed is *tlaa*, not *tlia*.

Sometimes the consonant can also be an /oo/ class consonant just like the sub-consonant. In this case, you simply base the vowel sound off of the /oo/ class.

e.g. គ (goo) + ្រ (jəəng roo) + ា (sra aa) = គ្រា (gria)

Here are some more examples of how words are formed with this class of subconsonants.

1. ថ្ងៃ (tngai) = ថ + ្ង + ៃ- (t + ng + ai)

2. ខ្ញុំ (kñom) = ខ + ្ញ + ំ (k + ñ + om)

3. ស្រា (sraa) = ស + ្រ- + -ា

(s + r + aa)

Some of these sub-consonants can change the sound of the uppercase consonant to which they are attached. First, if ក $gɔɔ$ is attached to a ្ *jəəng noo* or a ្ *jəəng moo*, then the consonant sound of ក changes from a /g/ to a /k/.

e.g. គ (goo) + ្ (jəəng noo) + ា (sra aa) = គ្ញា (knia)

ក (gɔɔ) + ្ (jəəng moo) + ្ (sra ua) + យ (yoo) = ក្មួយ (kmuay)

If a *jəəng roo* is added to a ប *bɔɔ*, then the sound of the ប changes from /b/ to a /bp/.

e.g. ប (bɔɔ) + ្រ (jəəng roo) + ៃ- (sra ai) = ប្រៃ (bprai)

ប (bɔɔ) + ្រ (jəəng roo) + ាំ (sra am) = ប្រាំ (bpram)

Reading Exercise: Read the following words with sub-consonants, and practice writing them in Cambodian.

1. ស្វាយ mango

2. ថ្ងៃ day

3. ខ្ញី ginger

4. ថ្ម rock

5. ស្លាប wing

6. ព្យូរ to hang

7. ថ្នាំ medication

8. ត្រី fish

9. ភ្ញៀវ guest

10. ស្លាក label

11. ក្នុង in

12. ប្រទេស country

Read and translate the following sentences.

1. ស្រុក ខ្មែរ នៅ ឆ្ងាយ ពី នេះ

2. គេ នៅ ក្នុង ផ្ទះ

3. ខ្ញុំ ទិញ ផ្ទៃឈើ នៅ ផ្សារ

4. លោក កំពុង ធ្វើ អ្វី

5. ខ្ញុំ មាន ស្វាយ និង ត្រី

6. ខ្ញុំ មាន ផ្ទាំ ច្រើន

7. គេ ចូលចិត្ត ទឹកក្រូច និង ស្រា

Writing Exercise 7

Transcribe the following into Cambodian script. These are all real Cambodian words. However, you may be able to phonetically spell them in several different ways.

1. svwet _____

2. sraek _____

3. slaak _____

4. a-vwey _____

5. bpyuh _____

6. tmeeñ _____

7. sliak _____

8. pnaek _____

9. bpruah _____

10. pñaɥ _____

11. srae _____

12. svwaeng _____

13. knong _____

14. bprɔ-tian _____

Lesson 8

Body parts; everyday life; more sub-consonants

mee-rian dtii bpram-bey មេរៀន ទី៨ **Lesson 8**

vɛak-a-sab វាក្យសព្ទ **Vocabulary**

ruub-gaay/kluan	រូបកាយ / ខ្លួន	body
sa-aat	ស្អាត	pretty, beautiful, clean
gbaal	ក្បាល	head
sɔk	សក់	hair
mok	មុខ	face
pnɛɛk	ភ្នែក	eye
jeñ-jaʉm	ចិញ្ចើម	eyebrow
room-pnɛɛk	រោមភ្នែក	eyelash
jrɔ-moh	ច្រមុះ	nose
moat	មាត់	mouth
bpuuk moat	ពុកមាត់	mustache
jɔɔng-gaa	ចង្កា	chin
bɔɔ-boo-moat	បបូរមាត់	lips
tmeeñ	ធ្មេញ	teeth
dtrɔ-jiak	ត្រចៀក	ear
gɔɔ	ក	neck
dtruung	ទ្រូង	chest
knɔɔng	ខ្នង	back
jɔng-geh	ចង្កេះ	lower back; waist
bpuah/grɔ-bpeah	ពោះ/ក្រពះ	stomach
gbaal-bpuah	ក្បាលពោះ	a fat stomach
dai	ដៃ	arm; hand
mriam-dai	ម្រាមដៃ	finger
grɔ-jɔɔk (dai)	ក្រចក (ដៃ)	fingernail
smaa	ស្មា	shoulder
jəəng	ជើង	foot; leg
mriam-jəəng	ម្រាមជើង	toe
jong-gong	ជង្គង់	knee
pləʉ	ភ្លៅ	thigh

sbaek ស្បែក	skin
kua-gbaal ខួរក្បាល	brain
beh-doong បេះដូង	heart
suat សួត	lung
tlaʉm ថ្លើម	liver
saik-dom សាច់ដុំ	muscle
cha-əng ឆ្អឹង	bone
chʉʉ ឈឺ	sick; to hurt
srual-kluan ស្រួលខ្លួន	to feel well
min srual-kluan មិនស្រួលខ្លួន	to not feel well
pdaa-saay ផ្ដាសាយ	cold; to have a cold
bpeet/gruu-bpeet ពេទ្យ / គ្រូពេទ្យ	doctor
tnam ថ្នាំ	medication
aaw អាវ	shirt
aaw-ro-ngia អាវរងា	jacket, coat
aaw-yʉʉt អាវយឺត	T-shirt
kao ខោ	pants
sɔm-bpot សំពត់	skirt
kao-aaw/sɔm-liak-bɔm-bpɛak ខោអាវ/សំលៀកបំពាក់	clothes[1]
muak មួក	hat
sbaek-jəəng ស្បែកជើង	shoes
sraom ស្រោម	a cylindrical covering
sraom-jəəng ស្រោមជើង	socks
sraom-dai ស្រោមដៃ	gloves
ksae-grɔ-vwat ខ្សែក្រវាត់	belt
jeñ-jian ចិញ្ចៀន	ring
ksae-dai ខ្សែដៃ	bracelet
sliak-bpɛak ស្លៀកពាក់	to wear
sliak ស្លៀក	to wear pants or a skirt[2]

bpɛak ពាក់	to wear something (except for pants and skirts)
dɔh ដោះ	to remove
dɔh kao-aaw ដោះខោអាវ	to take off clothing
dɔh sbaek-jəəng ដោះស្បែកជើង	to take off shoes
baok kao-aaw បោកខោអាវ	to wash clothes, do laundry
set sɔk សិតសក់	to comb hair
gao កោ	to shave
doh tmeeñ ដុសធ្មេញ	to brush teeth
muik-dtək មុជទឹក	to bathe
saa-buu សាប៊ូ	soap
liang លាង	to wash
sɔm-aat សំអាត	to clean
sɔm-aat pdtɛah សំអាតផ្ទះ	to clean the house
gɔk sɔk កក់សក់	to wash your hair
jaan ចាន	dishes
liang jaan លាងចាន	to wash dishes
dtrəᴐw ត្រូវ	to need to do something
dtrəᴐw-gaa ត្រូវការ	to need something
bpɔñ-ña-haa បញ្ហា	problem
...haᴐy (rᴐᴐ) nəᴐ? ...ហើយ(ឬ)នៅ?	...yet?[3]
dtoan ទាន់	in time, on time
min-dtoan មិនទាន់	not in time, not on time
nəᴐ lauy នៅឡើយ	not yet
tmey ថ្មី	new
jah ចាស់	old

Note: 1. sɔm-liak-bɔm-bpeak is more formal than kao-aaw.

2. sliak refers only to wearing pants or skirts. The word bpɛak should be used when referring to wearing anything else.

3. Colloquial speech usually omits the rᴐᴐ.

vwee-jia-gɔɔ   វេយ្យាករណ៍   **Grammar**

The words *dtrəuw* and *dtrəuw-gaa* are very important in the Cambodian language. Both words translate to the English verb "to need," but they are both used in different ways. *dtrəuw* means "to need to do something." It demands an action, not an object.

e.g. kñom dtrəuw dtəu psaa. = I need to go to the market.

In contrast, *dtrəuw-gaa* means "to need something." It demands an object, not an action.

e.g. kñom dtrəuw-gaa mhoob. = I need food.

This chapter also teaches how to ask if something is done yet and give a reply. The phrase *hauy-ruu-nəu* is placed at the end of a verb phrase to ask if that phrase has been accomplished yet or not.

e.g. dtau bong dtiñ siaw-pəu hauy ruu nəu? =
Have you bought the book yet?

Common speech often drops the ruu.

e.g. bɔɔng gɔk sɔk hauy-nəu? = Have you washed your hair yet?

A negative response uses *min dtoan* to indicate that it has not yet been accomplished. The word *nəu* at the beginning of the sentence is optional, and it serves as a quick answer to show that it has not yet been accomplished. *nəu lauy* is also an optional phrase used at the end of a negative response.

e.g. (nəu,) kñom min dtoan dtiñ vwia (nəu lauy) dtee. =
(No,) I have not yet bought it.

A positive response is shown by using the word *hauy* at the end of the sentence to show that it has already been accomplished.

e.g. baat, kñom dtiñ hauy. =
Yes, I bought it already.

The words *dtoan* and *min dtoan* can indicate whether or not something is done in or on time.

e.g. kñom tvwəə dtoan. = I did it in time.

e.g. kñom tvwəə min dtoan. = I did not get it done in time.

This chapter also introduces many verb phrases and other vocabulary that can be inserted into previously learned sentence structure.

e.g. kñom jɔng dɔh sbaek jəəng. =
I want to take my shoes off.
kñom min jɔng liang jaan dtee. =
I don't want to wash the dishes.

<u>Conversation</u>

Ryan: bɔɔng so-kim-naa sok-sɔb-baay dtee?
រីអាន បង សុយិមណា សុខសប្បាយ ទេ
How are you doing, Sokimna?

Sokimna: kñom min sǝʉw srual kluan.
សុយិមណា ខ្ញុំ មិន សូវ ស្រួល ខ្លួន
I don't feel very well.

Ryan: bɔɔng chʉʉ?
រីអាន បង ឈឺ
Are you sick?

Sokimna: jaa, kñom chʉʉ. haʉy tngai nih kñom dtrǝʉw
sɔm-aat pdtɛah dae.
សុយិមណា ចា៎ ខ្ញុំ ឈឺ ហើយ ថ្ងៃ នេះ ខ្ញុំ ត្រូវ
សំអាត ផ្ទះ ដែរ
Yes, I'm sick. I have to clean the house today too.

Ryan: min-ey-dtee. kñom aaik juay sɔm-aat pdtɛah
baan.
រីអាន មិនអីទេ ខ្ញុំ អាច ជួយ សំអាត ផ្ទះ
បាន
That's okay. I can help clean the house.

Sokimna: ɔɔ-gun.
សុយិមណា អរគុណ
Thank you.

Ryan: min-ey-dtee. min bɔñ-ña-haa dtee bɔɔng.
ñam tnam haʉy-nǝʉ?
រីអាន មិនអីទេ មិន បញ្ហា ទេ បង
ញ៉ាំ ថ្នាំ ហើយនៅ
That's okay. It's no problem at all. Have you
taken any medication yet?

Sokimna:	nəʉ. kñom min dtoan ñam tnam dtee.
សុឃិមណា	នៅ ខ្ញុំ មិន ទាន់ ញ៉ាំ ថ្នាំ ទេ
	No. I haven't taken anything yet.
Ryan:	ñam tnam haʉy sɔm-raak dtəʉ.[1]
រ៉្រៀអាន	ញ៉ាំ ថ្នាំ ហើយ សម្រាក ទៅ
	Go take some medication and get some rest.
Sokimna:	jaa. ɔɔ-gun.
សុឃិមណា	ចា៎ អរគុណ
	Okay. Thank you.

Note: 1. Here *dtəʉ* is placed at the end of the sentence to give a figurative meaning of "go ahead"or to go do something quickly.

klia ឃ្លា **Sentences**

1. A: dtau look dtrəuw tvwəə a-vwey klah dae?
   តើ លោក ត្រូវ ធ្វើ អ្វី ខ្លះ ដែរ
   What do you have to do?

   B: kñom dtrəuw aan siaw-pəu, liang laan, hauy
   sɔm-aat bɔn-dtub-dtək.
   ខ្ញុំ ត្រូវ អាន សៀវភៅ លាង ឡាន ហើយ
   សំអាត បន្ទប់ទឹក
   I need to read a book, wash the car, and clean the
   bathroom.

   C: kñom dtrəuw dtəu psaa maong bpii.
   ខ្ញុំ ត្រូវ ទៅ ផ្សារ ម៉ោង ពីរ
   I need to go to the market at 2:00.

   D: kñom dtrəuw dtiñ laan bpoa kmau.
   ខ្ញុំ ត្រូវ ទិញ ឡាន ពណ៌ ខ្មៅ
   I need to buy a black car.

2. A: dtau look dtrəuw-gaa a-vwey klah?
   តើ លោក ត្រូវការ អ្វី ខ្លះ
   What do you need?

   B: kñom dtrəuw-gaa laan tmey.
   ខ្ញុំ ត្រូវការ ឡាន ថ្មី
   I need a new car.

   C: kñom dtrəuw-gaa sɔɔm nəng slab-bpria.
   ខ្ញុំ ត្រូវការ សម និង ស្លាបព្រា
   I need a fork and spoon.

3. A: goat baok kao-aaw hauy-ruu-nəu?
   គាត់ បោក ខោអាវ ហើយឬនៅ
   Has he done the laundry yet?

B: (nəɯ), goat min dtoan baok kao-aaw dtee.
(នៅ) គាត់ មិន ទាន់ បោក ខោអាវ ទេ
(No), he has not yet done the laundry.

C: baat, goat baok kao-aaw haɯy.
បាទ គាត់ បោក ខោអាវ ហើយ
Yes, he has already done the laundry.

4.   A: goat mook dɔl haɯy-rɯɯ-nəɯ?
គាត់ មក ដល់ ហើយឬនៅ
Is he here yet?

B: baat, goat mook dɔl haɯy.
បាទ គាត់ មក ដល់ ហើយ
Yes, he is already here.

C: goat min dtoan mook dɔl nəɯ laɯy dtee.
គាត់ មិន ទាន់ មក ដល់ នៅ ឡើយ ទេ
He is not here yet.

5.   A: bɔɔng liang jaan dtoan dtee?
បង លាង ចាន ទាន់ ទេ
Did you wash the dishes in time?

B: kñom liang dtoan.
ខ្ញុំ លាង ទាន់
I washed them in time.

C: kñom liang min dtoan dtee.
ខ្ញុំ លាង មិន ទាន់ ទេ
I didn't wash them in time.

6.   A: dtaɯ bɔɔng dtəɯ dɔl dtoan dtee?
តើ បង ទៅ ដល់ ទាន់ ទេ
Did you get there on time?

B: kñom dtəɯ dɔl dtoan.
ខ្ញុំ ទៅ ដល់ ទាន់
I got there on time.

C: kñom dtəɯ dɔl ɔt dtoan.
ខ្ញុំ ទៅ ដល់ អត់ ទាន់
I didn't get there on time.

7. A: dtau goat sliak-bpɛak a-vwey klah?
       តើ គាត់ ស្លៀកពាក់ អ្វី ខ្លះ
       What is she wearing?

    B: goat sliak sɔm-bpot bpoa kiaw hauy bpɛak aaw bpoa
       sɔɔ.
       គាត់ ស្លៀក សំពត់ ពណិ ខៀវ ហើយ ពាក់ អាវ ពណិ
       ស
       She is wearing a blue skirt and a white shirt.

    C: goat sliak kao bpoa kmau.
       គាត់ ស្លៀក ខោ ពណិ ខ្មៅ
       She is wearing black pants.

    D: goat bpɛak aaw bpoa grɔ-hɔɔm.
       គាត់ ពាក់ អាវ ពណិ ក្រហម
       She is wearing a red shirt.

8. A: dtau bɔɔng srual-kluan dtee?
       តើ បង ស្រួលខ្លួន ទេ
       Are you feeling well?

    B: jaa, kñom srual-kluan.
       ចា៎ ខ្ញុំ ស្រួលខ្លួន
       Yes, I am feeling well.

    C: dtee. kñom min sǝuw srual-kluan dtee.
       ទេ ខ្ញុំ មិន សូវ ស្រួលខ្លួន ទេ
       No, I am not feeling very well.

    D: kñom chuu gbaal.
       ខ្ញុំ ឈឺ ក្បាល
       I have a headache.

    E: kñom chuu bpuah.
       ខ្ញុំ ឈឺ ពោះ
       I have a stomachache.

    F: kñom chuu beh-doong.
       ខ្ញុំ ឈឺ បេះដូង
       I have a heart disorder.

Drills

1. Practice saying the following sentences in Cambodian. If the sentence is a question, practice answering it as well.

I have to go to the bathroom.

_____

Did Bob wash the dishes yet?

_____

2. Do the following.

Describe what you are wearing in spoken Cambodian.

Practice saying the common nursery rhyme "Head, Shoulders, Knees, and Toes" in Cambodian. This will help you remember the Cambodian words for the parts of the body. For those who may be unfamiliar with the rhyme, you name the following body parts in this order while touching them with your fingers: "Head, shoulders, knees, and toes; knees and toes; knees and toes; head, shoulders, knees, and toes; eyes, ears, mouth, and nose."

3. Use the following words to help form ten sentences.

kñom	dtoan	jaan
min	baok kao-aaw	pdtɛah
sliak	bpoa	tmey
haɥy	dtiñ	kao
aaw	muak	grɔ-hɔɔm
kmau	bpɛak	goat
gbaal	srual-kluan	sɔm-bpot
haɥy-rɥɥ-nəɥ	bpuah	bɔɔng
dtee	nəɥ-laɥy	dtəɥ
liang	tvwəə	muik-dtək
dtrəɥw-gaa	dtee	dtrəɥw

Test 8

Match the English words with the Cambodian words.

_____ 1. clothes   a. sɔm-bpot   សំពត់

_____ 2. sick   b. liang   លាង

_____ 3. skirt   c. sbaek   ស្បែក

_____ 4. face   d. sɔm-liak-bɔm-bpɛak   សំលៀកបំពាក់

_____ 5. skin   e. sɔk   សក់

_____ 6. to wash   f. aaw   អាវ

_____ 7. arm   g. tlaɥm   ថ្លើម

_____ 8. eyes   h. kua-gbaal   ខួរក្បាល

_____ 9. brain   i. dai   ដៃ

_____ 10. hair   j. mok   មុខ

_____ 11. liver   k. pnɛɛk   ភ្នែក

_____ 12. shirt   l. jəəng   ជើង

                     m. chɥɥ   ឈឺ

                     n. sraom   ស្រោម

Translate the following into English or Cambodian.

1. goat mook pdtɛah vwiñ haɐy-nəɐ?

   គាត់   មក   ផ្ទះ   វិញ   ហើយនៅ

   _____

2. kñom sliak-bpɛak aaw bpoa sɔɔ nəng kao bpoa kiaw.

   ខ្ញុំ   ស្លៀកពាក់   អាវ   ពណ៌   ស   និង   ខោ   ពណ៌   ខៀវ

   _____

3. kñom chɐɐ jɔng-geh.

   ខ្ញុំ   ឈឺ   ចង្កេះ

   _____

4. I need new clothes.

   _____

5. His hat is too big.

   _____

Sub-Consonants ជើង jəəng

This last set of sub-consonants is unique. All are either silent, seldom used, or obsolete.

Consonant	Pronunciation	Sound
្ឋ	too	/t/[1]
្ឍ	tɔɔ	/t/[1]
្ណ	nɔɔ	/n/[1]
្បៗ	koo	/k/[2]
្ឝ	choo	/ch/[2]
្ឈ	chɔɔ	/ch/[2]
្ឈៗ	too	/t/[3]
្ឌ	doo	/d/[2]
្ឋ	pɔɔ	/p/[3]

Note: 1. These sub-consonants are used seldomly. They are oftentimes used as final silent sub-consonants.
2. These sub-consonants are used seldomly.
3. These sub-consonants are completely obsolete and seldom if ever used.

Practice Writing Lowercase Consonants

Use ñ /-/ as the consonant when practicing the following lower-case consonants.

គឺ	គឺ	គឺ	គឺ	គឺ

គេ	គេ	គេ	គេ	គេ

gaa-bpon-yul ការពន្យល់ **Explanation**

In written Cambodian, it is sometimes common to have a final sub-consonant on a word that is silent. It emits no sound, but it is placed there anyway. There are also other sub-consonants besides the three identified in this chapter that can be placed at the end of a word and emit no sound. The general rule is that if there is a sub-consonant at the very end of a word, it is unpronounced.

e.g. រាជ្ជ (roat) $=$ រ $+$ ជ $+$ $\underset{\smile}{-}$ (roa+t $+$ t)[1,2]

ស៊ុទ្ធ (sot) $=$ ស $+\underset{\shortmid}{-}+$ ទ $+$ $\underset{\smile}{-}$ (s $+$ o $+$ t $+$ t)[1]

ពេទ្យ (bpeet) $=$ ព $+$ េ $+$ ទ $-$ យ (bp+ee $+$ t $+$ y)[1]

Note: 1. Remember that the final consonant sound resulting from the sub-consonant is silent.
       2. Please note that this word has an irregular vowel sound that does not follow proper phonetics.

Reading Exercise: Read the following words, and practice writing them in Cambodian.

1. រដ្ឋ   state

2. មិត្ត   friend

3. បញ្ឆោត to trick, deceive[1]

4. ចិត្ត   heart

5. សង្ឃ   monk

6. សុទ្ធ   pure

7. ចក្រ   kingdom

8. សង្ឃឹម hope

Note: 1. The wavy line on the bottom of the ញ /ñoo/ character is dropped when a sub-consonant is placed beneath it.

Read the following sentences aloud, and rewrite them.

1. ខ្ញុំ សង្ឃឹម ថា បង មាន លុយ

2. សុផា ស្វៀក ខោ ស

3. ខ្ញុំ ត្រូវការ ឡាន ស្អាត

4. ក្រូពេទ្យ មាន សាប៊ូ និង ថ្នាំ

5. ខ្ញុំ បាន ជួប គេ នៅ រដ្ឋ នេះ

Writing Exercise 8

Translate the following English sentences and write them in Cambodian script.

1. I am wearing a blue jacket and white shirt.

2. The doctor has a big house.

3. I have a toothache.

4. Tim needs to shave his mustache.

5. Who is going to clean the bathroom?

Lesson 9

Comparisons; classifiers; more adjectives;
other features of written Cambodian

mee-rian dtii bpram-buan មេរៀន ទី៩ Lesson 9

vɛak-a-sab វាក្យសព្ទ Vocabulary

bproh	ប្រុស	male, boy, man
srey	ស្រី	female, girl, woman
gɔng	កង់	bicycle
dtɛang	ទាំង	plural particle
jiang	ជាង	more, greater
jiang-gee	ជាងគេ	most, greatest
jiang-gee bɔm-pot	ជាងគេបំផុត	absolute most, greatest
dooik	ដូច	alike, similar
min dooik	មិនដូច	unlike, dissimilar
dooik-knia	ដូចគ្នា	same[1]
min dooik-knia	មិនដូចគ្នា	not the same[1]
dtae	តែ	only
dtae-bpon-nɔh	តែប៉ុណ្ណោះ	only (final particle)
bprɔɔ-hael (jia)	ប្រហែល (ជា)	about, approximately; maybe
sgoom	ស្គម	skinny
toat	ធាត់	fat
grah	ក្រាស់	thick
sdaung	ស្តើង	thin
tngon	ធ្ងន់	heavy
sraal	ស្រាល	light
dtom-ngon	ទម្ងន់	weight
kbpuah	ខ្ពស់	tall, high
dtiab	ទាប	short
gɔm-bpuah	កំពស់	height
klang	ខ្លាំង	strong
ksaoy	ខ្សោយ	weak

gdau ក្ដៅ		hot
dtrɔ-jɛak ត្រជាក់		cold
ro-ngia រងា		cool, chilly, cold
plɯɯ ភ្លឺ		bright
ngo-ngət ងងឹត		dark
yook-jet-dtuk-dak យកចិត្តទុកដាក់		to be diligent[2]
kjil ខ្ជិល		lazy
riab រាប		flat
ro-lɛak រលាក់		bumpy
snguat ស្ងួត		dry
dto-dtək/saɯm ទទឹក / សើម		wet
bprɔ-lak ប្រឡាក់		dirty, soiled
ɔh-jaa អស្ចារ្យ		awesome, great, magnificent
ɔn អន់		poor, inadequate
mian មាន		wealthy, rich
grɔɔ ក្រ		poor, impoverished
kooik ខូច		broken; naughty; dead

Note: 1. Cambodian also has the phrase *koh-knia* which means "different."

2. The only way to express diligence is to use a verb phrase.
   e.g. *kñom yook-jet-dtuk-dak tvwəə-gaa.* = "I work diligently."

Classifiers

Classifiers are specific words which are used to identify nouns. The Cambodian language uses classifiers quite frequently for some words, but they are also oftentimes omitted. English also has classifiers (*rolls* of paper, *glasses* of water, *pairs* of shoes, etc.)

Below we have listed some of the most common classifiers in the Cambodian language and what they are used for.

Classifier		Common Use of Classifier
nek	នាក់	people
sɔn-lək	សន្លឹក	flat things, sheets of paper
gbaal	ក្បាល	books and animals
dɔɔng	ដង	number of times, occurances
dom	ដុំ	chunk, piece, bunch, roll
jaan	ចាន	plates of food, servings
gaew	កែវ	glasses of water, soda, etc.
dɔɔb	ដប	bottles of water, soda, etc.
gɔm-bpong	កំប៉ុង	cans of soda, juice, etc.
guu	គូ	pairs of things
gruang	គ្រឿង	machines
groab	គ្រាប់	small round things (pills, pieces of candy, seeds, etc.)
joan	ជាន់	floor, level, story
yaang	យ៉ាង	ways, kinds, types
bɔn-dtub	បន្ទប់	rooms
ruang	រឿង	stories, movies
jbab	ច្បាប់	documents, letters, copies
jɔm-net	ចំណិត	slices
daum	ដើម	sticks, guns, long and thin objects
gii-loo	គីឡូ	kilograms

maet ម៉ែត្រ	meters
gii-loo-maet គីឡូម៉ែត្រ	kilometers
baaw បាវ	large bags of something (usually used with bags of rice)
gɔm-plee កំប្លេ	sets of clothes (top and bottom)
mat ម៉ាត់	mouthful, words
gəm-noo គំនរ	large groups, piles
sɔɔ-sai សរសៃ	strands, threads

vwee-jia-gɔɔ   វេយ្យាករណ៍   **Grammar**

Comparisons are introduced in this chapter. They are an extremely useful part of Cambodian speech. The key word for comparisons is *jiang*. This word is also always used with a modifier. The modifier comes first.

e.g. laan nih tom jiang. = This car is bigger.

jiang is also used to compare two objects in the same sentence.

e.g. laan nih tom jiang laan nuh. = This car is bigger than that car.

When *jiang-gee* is combined with a modifier, it forms a superlative.

e.g. laan nih tom jiang-gee. = This is the biggest car.

The word *bɔm-pot* can be added to indicate an even higher superlative.

e.g. laan nih tom jiang-gee bɔm-pot. = This is the absolute biggest car.

This chapter introduces classifiers. Normally classifiers come at the end of sentences or phrases in this manner.

(noun) - (modifier) - (classifier)

e.g. sbaek-jəəng bpii guu = Two pairs of shoes

Cambodian also uses classifiers in some situations where classifiers are not typically used in English.

e.g. tnam bey groab = Three pills

Classifiers can then be put into a sentence structure.

e.g. kñom jɔng dtiñ dtək-krooik bpii dɔɔb. = I want to buy two bottles of soda.

dooik means "alike" or "similar." It is used much like it is used in English.

e.g. aaw nih min dooik aaw kñom dtee. = This shirt is not like my shirt.

dooik-knia means "the same."

e.g. aaw nih nəng aaw nuh dooik-knia. = This shirt and that shirt are the same.

Conversation

Sambat: dtau bɔɔng jɔng ñam dtək plae-chəə ruu dtee?
សម្បត្តិ តើ បង ចង់ ញ៉ាំ ទឹក ផ្លែឈើ ឬ ទេ
Would you like to drink some fruit juice?

Jill: jaa, ɔɔ-gun.
ជិល ចាំ អរគុណ
Yes, thank you.

Sambat: tom-mdaa, bɔɔng jool-jet ñam dtək a-vwey dae?
សម្បត្តិ ធម្មតា បង ចូលចិត្ត ញ៉ាំ ទឹក អ្វី ដែរ
What do you normally like to drink?

Jill: kñom jool-jet ñam dtək-krooik.
ជិល ខ្ញុំ ចូលចិត្ត ញ៉ាំ ទឹក ក្រូច
I like to drink soda.

Sambat: knong muay tngai ñam bpon-maan gɔm-bpong?
សម្បត្តិ ក្នុង មួយ ថ្ងៃ ញ៉ាំ ប៉ុន្មាន កំប៉ុង
How many cans do you drink in a day?

Jill: knong muay tngai, kñom ñam dtək-grooik
bprɔ-hael-jia bpii ruu bey gɔm-bpong.
ជិល ក្នុង មួយ ថ្ងៃ ខ្ញុំ ញ៉ាំ ទឹកក្រូច
ប្រហែលជា ពីរ ឬ បី កំប៉ុង
I drink maybe two or three cans a day.

Sambat: kñom jool-jet ñam dtək-krooik, bpon-dtae kñom
git taa dtək-plae-chəə chngañ jiang.
សម្បត្តិ ខ្ញុំ ចូលចិត្ត ញ៉ាំ ទឹកក្រូច ប៉ុន្តែ ខ្ញុំ
គិត ថា ទឹកផ្លែឈើ ឆ្ងាញ់ ជាង
I like to drink soda, but I think that fruit juice
tastes better.

Jill: kñom jool-jet ñam dtək-grooik bpruah vwia
                taok jiang dtək-plae-chəə.

ជិល   ខ្ញុំ   ចូលចិត្ត ញ៉ាំ   ទឹកក្រូច   ព្រោះ   វា
                ថោក   ជាង   ទឹកផ្លែឈើ

                I like to drink soda because it is cheaper than fruit
                juice.

Sambat: baat, dtək-grooik taok jiang mɛɛn.

សម្បត្តិ   បាទ   ទឹកក្រូច   ថោក   ជាង   មែន

                Yeah, soda really is cheaper.

klia ឃ្លា **Sentences**

1. A: sbaek-jəəng kmau sa-aat jiang sbaek jəəng grɔ-hɔɔm.
   ស្បែកជើង ខៅ ស្អាត ជាង ស្បែកជើង ក្រហម
   Black shoes are prettier than red shoes.

   B: sbaek-jəəng kmau min sa-aat jiang sbaek-jəəng
   grɔ-hɔɔm dtee.
   ស្បែកជើង ខៅ មិន ស្អាត ជាង ស្បែកជើង
   ក្រហម ទេ
   Black shoes are not prettier than red shoes.

   C: sbaek-jəəng kmau sa-aat jiang-gee.
   ស្បែកជើង ខៅ ស្អាត ជាងគេ
   Black shoes are the prettiest.

2. A: dtaʉ pia-saa muay naa bpi-baak jiang, pia-saa
   ɔng-glee rʉʉ pia-saa kmae?
   តើ ភាសា មួយ ណា ពិបាក ជាង ភាសា
   អង់គ្លេស ឬ ភាសា ខ្មែរ
   Which language is more difficult, English or
   Cambodian?

   B: pia-saa ɔng-glee bpi-baak jiang pia-saa kmae.
   ភាសា អង់គ្លេស ពិបាក ជាង ភាសា ខ្មែរ
   English is more difficult than Cambodian.

   C: pia-saa ɔng-glee min bpi-baak jiang pia-saa kmae
   dtee.
   ភាសា អង់គ្លេស មិន ពិបាក ជាង ភាសា ខ្មែរ
   ទេ
   English is not more difficult than Cambodian.

   D: pia-saa kmae bpi-baak jiang.
   ភាសា ខ្មែរ ពិបាក ជាង
   Cambodian is more difficult.

E: pia-saa kmae bpi-baak jiang-gee.
ភាសា ខ្មែរ ពិបាក ជាងគេ
Cambodian is the most difficult.

3. A: dtau bɔɔng jool-jet muak muay naa jiang.
តើ បង ចូលចិត្ត មួក មួយ ណា ជាង
Which hat do you like more?

B: kñom jool-jet muak nih jiang.
ខ្ញុំ ចូលចិត្ត មួក នេះ ជាង
I like this hat more.

4. A: kao muay naa bprɔ-lak jiang?
ខោ មួយ ណា ប្រឡាក់ ជាង
Which pair of pants are dirtier?

B: kao nuh bprɔ-lak jiang.
ខោ នោះ ប្រឡាក់ ជាង
Those pants are dirtier.

5. A: dtau look mian grɔ-dah bpon-maan sɔn-lək?
តើ លោក មាន ក្រដាស ប៉ុន្មាន សន្លឹក
How many sheets of paper do you have?

B: kñom mian grɔ-dah buan sɔn-lək.
ខ្ញុំ មាន ក្រដាស បួន សន្លឹក
I have four sheets of paper.

6. A: dtau goat ñam mhoob kmae bpon-maan jaan dae?
តើ គាត់ ញ៉ាំ ម្ហូប ខ្មែរ ប៉ុន្មាន ចាន ដែរ
How many servings of Cambodian food did he eat?

B: goat ñam mhoob kmae bpii jaan.
គាត់ ញ៉ាំ ម្ហូប ខ្មែរ ពីរ ចាន
He ate two servings of Cambodian food.

7. kñom mian pdtɛah bey joan.
ខ្ញុំ មាន ផ្ទះ បី ជាន់
I have a three story house.

8. so-vwan mian dtom-ngon sae-seb gii-loo.
សុវណ្ណ មាន ទម្ងន់ សែសិប គីឡូ
Sovann weighs forty kilograms.

9.   kñom dtəu srok kmae bpii dɔɔng hauy.
           ខ្ញុំ ទៅ ស្រុក ខ្មែរ ពីរ ដង ហើយ
           I have been to Cambodia two times already.

10.   A: dtau look ñam tnam bpon-maan groab hauy?
           តើ លោក ញ៉ាំ ថ្នាំ ប៉ុន្មាន គ្រាប់ ហើយ
           How many pills did you take?

      B: kñom ñam bey groab hauy.
           ខ្ញុំ ញ៉ាំ បី គ្រាប់ ហើយ
           I took three pills.

11.   goat mian bpuak-maak jraun nek.
           គាត់ មាន ពួកម៉ាក ច្រើន នាក់
           She has a lot of friends.

12.   kñom mian siaw-pəu jraun jiang-gee.
           ខ្ញុំ មាន សៀវភៅ ច្រើន ជាងគេ
           I have the most books.

13.   A: dtau bprɔ-dteeh muay naa gdau jiang-gee?
           តើ ប្រទេស មួយ ណា ក្ដៅ ជាងគេ
           Which country is the hottest.

      B: bprɔ-dteeh kmae gdau jiang-gee.
           ប្រទេស ខ្មែរ ក្ដៅ ជាងគេ
           Cambodia the is the hottest.

14.   srok kmae jia srok gdau jiang-gee bɔm-pot.
           ស្រុក ខ្មែរ ជា ស្រុក ក្ដៅ ជាងគេ បំផុត
           Cambodia is the absolute hottest country.

15.   A: sbaek-jəəng dtɛang nih dooik-knia dtee?
           ស្បែកជើង ទាំង នេះ ដូចគ្នា ទេ
           Are these shoes the same?

      B: jaa, dooik-knia.
           ចាំ ដូចគ្នា
           Yes, they are the same.

      C: min dooik-knia dtee.
           មិន ដូចគ្នា ទេ
           They are not the same.

16. A: aaw nih nəng aaw nuh dooik-knia.
     អាវ នេះ និង អាវ នោះ ដូចគ្នា
     This shirt and that shirt are the same.

     B: aaw nih nəng aaw nuh min dooik-knia dtee.
     អាវ នេះ និង អាវ នោះ មិន ដូចគ្នា ទេ
     This shirt and that shirt are not the same.

17. pləɯw dtɛang bpii nih ro-lɛak dooik-knia.
     ផ្លូវ ទាំង ពីរ នេះ រលាក់ ដូចគ្នា
     Both of these roads are equally bumpy.

18. srey nəɯ srok nih min dooik srey nəɯ srok kñom dtee.
     ស្រី នៅ ស្រុក នេះ មិន ដូច ស្រី នៅ ស្រុក ខ្ញុំ ទេ
     The girls here are not like the girls in my country.

19. gɔng nih min səɯw tngon dooik gɔng kñom dtee.
     កង់ នេះ មិន សូវ ធ្ងន់ ដូច កង់ ខ្ញុំ ទេ
     This bike is not as heavy as my bike.

Drills

1. Practice saying the following sentences in Cambodian.

   I have two glasses of water.

   _____

   My bag is lighter than your bag.

   _____

   2. Do one of the following.

   Compare two objects in Cambodian. You must say which one is better and give at least two reasons why using the word *jiang*.

   Say in Cambodian what you had (or will have) for all your meals today. You must give the food, drink, and amount of servings. Classifiers must be used.

3. Use the following words to help form ten sentences with classifiers.

kñom	tnam	gbaal
jaan	joan	pdtɛah
muay	jbab	sɔn-lək
gaew	dtiñ	goat
mhoob	mian	dtək
siaw-pəʉ	saam-seb	kao-aaw
gii-loo	gɔm-plee	goat
bey	buan	dtom-ngon
groab	ñam	grɔ-dah

Test 9

Match the English words with the Cambodian words.

_____ 1. strong   a. kjil ខ្ជិល

_____ 2. lazy   b. sraal ស្រាល

_____ 3. poor   c. gdau ក្ដៅ

_____ 4. maybe   d. saʉm សើម

_____ 5. incredible   e. snguat ស្ងួត

_____ 6. short   f. dtiab ទាប

_____ 7. flat   g. klang ខ្លាំង

_____ 8. hot   h. ɔh-jaa អស្ចារ្យ

_____ 9. light   i. bprɔɔ-hael ប្រហែល

_____ 10. dry   j. grɔɔ ក្រ

                               k. riab រាប

Match the Cambodian words with their appropriate classifier.

_____ 1. movie   a. jaan ចាន

_____ 2. letter   b. baaw បាវ

_____ 3. serving   c. joan ជាន់

_____ 4. sheet of paper   d. dɔɔb ដប

_____ 5. floor   e. rʉang រឿង

_____ 6. times, occurances   f. guu គូ

_____ 7. people   g. dɔɔng ដង

_____ 8. bag   h. maet ម៉ែត្រ

_____ 9. shoes   i. nek នាក់

_____ 10. bottle   j. sɔn-lək សន្លឹក

                               k. jbab ច្បាប់

Numbers   លេខ   leek

The last set of characters to learn in the Cambodian alphabet is the Cambodian script for numbers. Normally in Cambodian writing, numbers can either be written through this script or spelled out phonetically. When making larger numbers, these characters are combined just like they are in English.

Consonant	Pronunciation	English
０	soon សូន	0
១	muay មួយ	1
២	bpii ពីរ	2
៣	bey បី	3
៤	buan បួន	4
៥	bpram ប្រាំ	5
៦	bpram-muay ប្រាំមួយ	6
៧	bpram-bpii/bpram-bpəl ប្រាំពីរ	7
៨	bpram-bey ប្រាំបី	8
៩	bpram-buan ប្រាំបួន	9

Practice Writing Numbers

0 0 0 0 0

១ ១ ១ ១ ១

២ ២ ២ ២ ២

៣ ៣ ៣ ៣ ៣

៤ ៤ ៤ ៤ ៤

៥ ៥ ៥ ៥ ៥

៦ ៦ ៦ ៦ ៦

៧ ៧ ៧ ៧ ៧

៨ ៨ ៨ ៨ ៨

៩ ៩ ៩ ៩ ៩

Other Features of Written Cambodian

You have now learned all of the characters in the Cambodian script. However, there are still other important parts of Cambodian writing that you need to study. You will now be introduced to the symbols used in Cambodian script as well as other features of written Cambodian. Symbols in written Cambodian are usually placed above a consonant and alter its natural or vowel sound.

1.　　　The mark ʼ *bɔn-dtɔk* is placed above final consonants, and affects the vowel sound of a word in several ways. First, this mark is often placed above a final consonant in a word with an initial /ɔɔ/ series consonant. There may or may not be a vowel, but the vowel sound is always long. When the *bɔn-dtɔk* is used in this manner, the *bɔn-dtɔk* changes the long vowel sound to a short vowel sound.

ចាក់　　　　　jak　　　　　to inject; to insert
កាត់　　　　　gat　　　　　to cut
ថត់　　　　　jɔt　　　　　bitter

Secondly, when a *bɔn-dtɔk* is placed above the final consonant in a word initiated with an /oo/ series consonant, the vowel sound can be affected in one of three ways. The first way is when there is no vowel in the word. In this case, the consonant's own vowel sound is simply changed from a long vowel sound to a short vowel sound.

ឈប់　　　　　chob　　　　　to stop
ទប់　　　　　dtob　　　　　to barricade, defend

If a *bɔn-dtɔk* is placed above a final ក (gɔɔ) in a word starting with an /oo/ series consonant and followed by a ា (sra-aa), the vowel sound changes to /ɛa/ in this manner.

ទាក់　　　　　dtɛak　　　　　to attract
ជាក់　　　　　jɛak　　　　　to clarify

ពាក់   bpɛak   to wear

Finally, if a *bɔn-dtɔk* is placed above any other final consonant in a word starting with an /oo/ series consonant and followed by a ា (sra-aa), the vowel sound changes to /oa/ in this manner.

ទាន់   dtoan   on time, in time
ជាន់   joan   floor; to step on
ទាត់   dtoat   to kick
ទាល់   dtoal   until

2.   The next mark is " and is called *tmeeñ gɔn-dao*. It literally means "rat's teeth" because of its appearance. This marking has two main purposes. First, when placed above an /oo/ series consonant, it changes the natural /oo/ vowel sound to an /ɔɔ/ vowel sound. If a vowel is added, the resulting vowel sound would be an /ɔɔ/ class vowel sound. This marking is also very useful when spelling foreign words such as names.

ម៉ត់ចត់   mɔt-jɔt   careful, carefully
រ៉ប់   rab   to guarantee; to take
                                   responsibility
រ៉ន   Ron   (foreign name)

This mark is also commonly used above the ប (bɔɔ) consonant. When placed above this consonant, the sound of the consoant changes from /b/ to /bp/.

ប៉ះ   bpah   to touch
ប៉ោម   bpaom   apple
ប៉ុណ្ណោះ   bpon-nɔh   only
ប៉ុស្តិ៍   bpoh   channel (radio, television)

3.   The ~ *dtrey-sab* mark does the opposite of the mark just introduced.   When placed above an /ɔɔ/ series consonant, it changes its natural /ɔɔ/ vowel sound to an /oo/ vowel sound. If a vowel is added, the resulting vowel sound would be an /oo/ class vowel sound.

| ហ៊ាន | hian | to dare; be brave |
| ក្រុមហ៊ុន | grom-hun | company |

Instead of using a ~ mark above the character, a ˌ mark below the character can also sometimes be used instead. It resembles a *sra-o* vowel, but in this case, it is not a vowel. When this marking is used, the vowel sound is altered the same way as with the original mark.

| អាស៊ី | aa-sii | Asia |
| ញ៉ាំ | ñam | to eat |

4.   The ៨ symbol resembles a small number eight. It is a silent character placed above two consonants: ក /gɔɔ/ and ដ /dɔɔ/. When placed above these consonants, each consonant becomes a particle which is very useful in the Cambodian language.

ក៏	gɔɔ	also, then, therefore
ក៏ប៉ុន្តែ	gɔɔ-bpon-dtae	however, but
ដ៏	dɔɔ	very (particle)
ដ៏ធំ	dɔɔ-tom	very big

5.   The ៏ symbol is placed above a consonant to indicate that the consonant should not be pronounced. In other words, it silences that consonant. This symbol also resembles a small number nine.

សាសន៍	saah	race, ethnicity
ទូរទស្សន៍	dtuu-rə-dtuah	television
សប្ដាហ៍	sa-bdaa	week

6.　　The ៑ symbol looks very similar to the previous symbol, but it is very different. This symbol is placed above a consonant to provide an /oa/ vowel sound. It is not used very frequently.

យុត្តិធម៌	yut-dte-toa	justice
ពតិមាន	bpoa-dɔ-mian	information, news
ធម៌	toa	generosity

7.　　The ៗ symbol is the repeater symbol. This means that it repeats the word directly before it. In Cambodian, when a word is repeated twice, it gives the word double emphasis.

ខ្លាំងៗ	klang-klang	*very* strong
គាត់ មាន ផ្ទះ ថ្មីៗ	goat mian pdtɛah tmey-tmey	
	He has a *brand* new house.	
ចាស់ៗ	jah-jah	*very* old

8.　　The ៝ symbol is sometimes placed above a consonant to produce a vowel sound. That consonant is usually followed by a យ /yoo/ consonant which provides the final consonant sound. When placed above a វ /vwoo/ or ន /noo/ consonant, it typically form an /e/ vowel sound.

| ន័យ | ney | meaning |
| វ័យ | vwey | age |

When the symbol is used with other consonants, it typically forms a short /a/ vowel sound.

បណ្ណាល័យ	ban-naa-lay	library
វិនិច្ឆ័យ	vwi-ni-chay	to judge
រហ័ស	la-hah	fast, quick
Sometimes it can also produces the /oa/ vowel sound.		
កងទ័ព	gɔng-dtoab	army
ទំព័រ	dəm-bpoa	page

9.   The ៈ symbol simply indicates a short /a/ vowel sound for /ɔɔ/ series consonants and an /ɛah/ vowel sound for /oo/ series consonants. This symbol is very similar to the /ៈ/ (sra-ah) vowel, but it is used much less frequently and has no final /h/ sound.

        គណៈ   ga-na   group
        សិល្បៈ   sel-la-ba   the fine arts

10.   The ៎ leek book symbol is very rare, but it is used to add an excited emphasis to a word, kind of like an English exclamation point.

        ណែ៎   nae   Hey!
        នុះន៎   nuh-nɔɔ   Over there!

11.   The ។ kan symbol is used as the equivalent to an English period. It is placed at the end of a sentence. When ending an entire story, another line is place to the right of the symbol to indicate that the story is over. (៕) The ។ symbol can also be used in combination with the character ល. When you see the combination ។ល។ , this is the Cambodian equivalent of the the English ecetera (etc.).

12.   The ៛ symbol is the symbol for Cambodia's currency: the Cambodian riel. It is usually placed after an amount instead of at the beginning.

        ៣000 ៛   bey-bpoan rial   three thousand riel

13.   Cambodia has also adopted punctuation marks from Western languages. The question mark (?), exclamation point (!), and slash mark (/) are sometimes used.

        ហេតុអ្វី?   haet a-vwey?   Why?
        កុំ!   gom!   Don't!

Writing Exercise 9

Read the following words, and write them in Cambodian. Use at least one of the symbols discussed above. There may be several ways to phonetically spell some of these words, but only the correct spelling is given in the answer guide.

Word	Meaning	Rewrite
1. dak	to place	_____
2. yaang	kind, variety	_____
3. sa-aat sa-aat	very beautiful	_____
4. bprɔ-sah	words, speech	_____
5. rɛak-dtɛak	to be friendly	_____
6. rong-vwoan	reward	_____
7. bpoa	color	_____
8. toa	generosity	_____
9. gɔt	to write down, record	_____
10. bik	pen	_____

11. bpon-dtae   but   _____

12. dtooik dtooik   very small   _____

13. gɔɔ-baan   all right, okay _____

14. sɔng-say   unsure   _____

15. mo-haa-vwi-dtyia-lay college   _____

Lesson 10

Family and kinship terms; occupations; animals;
the many forms of the word "you"

mee-rian dtii dɔb មេរៀន ទី១០ Lesson 10

vɛak-a-sab វាក្យសព្ទ Vocabulary

sɔɔb-baay-jet	សប្បាយចិត្ត	happy
bpi-baak-jet	ពិបាកចិត្ត	sad, troubled
kooik-jet	ខូចចិត្ត	heartbroken
jrɔ-lɔm	ច្រឡំ	confused
ɔh-gam-lang	អស់កម្លាំង	exhausted
(ngo) nguy-geeng	(ង)ងុយគេង	sleepy
rəm-pəəb	រំភើប	excited
chguat	ឆ្កួត	crazy
koo-kəн	យោយៅ	cruel, savage
sɔm-kan	សំខាន់	important
riab-gaa/gaa	រៀបការ/ការ	to marry, married
liiw	លីវ	single
sɔɔng-saa	សង្សារ	steady girlfriend/ boyfriend, lover
ro-bɔh	របស់	particle that shows possession
aeng	ឯង	oneself
kluan-aeng	ខ្លួនឯង	by oneself
mnek-aeng	ម្នាក់ឯង	alone
mook mneak-aeng	មកម្នាក់ឯង	to come alone
tvwəə-jia	ធ្វើជា	to be something
sɔb-tngai nih	សព្ថ្ងៃនេះ	nowadays
jia-bprɔɔ-jam	ជាប្រចាំ	regularly
bprɔɔ-jam tngai	ប្រចាំថ្ងៃ	daily
bprɔɔ-jam kae	ប្រចាំខែ	monthly
bprɔɔ-jam chnam	ប្រចាំឆ្នាំ	yearly
roal	រាល់	every
piak-jraнn	ភាគច្រើន	mostly, majority

piak-dtek ភាគតិច		small percentage, minority
dtii/dtii-gɔn-laeng/gɔn-laeng ទី/ទីកន្លែង/កន្លែង		place
ei-ləɯw (nih) ឥឡូវ (នេះ)		right now, this second
daoy ដោយ		through, by means of

grua-saa ត្រួសារ **Family**

ow-bpuk ឪពុក	father
mdaay ម្ដាយ	mother
bdey ប្ដី	husband
bprɔɔ-bpon ប្រពន្ធ	wife
bɔɔng-ba-oon បងប្អូន	siblings, family
bɔɔng-bproh បងប្រុស	older brother
bɔɔng-srey បងស្រី	older sister
bɔ-oon-bproh ប្អូនប្រុស	younger brother
bɔ-oon-srey ប្អូនស្រី	younger sister
goon កូន	child
goon-bproh កូនប្រុស	son
goon-srey កូនស្រី	daughter
goon-bɔɔng-gee កូនបងគេ	oldest sibling
goon-bpəɯ កូនពៅ	youngest sibling
bpuu ពូ	uncle
ming មីង	aunt
bɔɔng-jii-doon-muay បងជីដូនមួយ	older cousin
bɔ-oon-jii-doon-muay ប្អូនជីដូនមួយ	younger cousin
dtaa/jii-dtaa តា / ជីតា	grandfather
yiay/jii-doon យាយ / ជីដូន	grandmother
dtaa-dtuat តាតួត	great-grandfather
yiay-dtuat យាយតួត	great-grandmother
kmuay ក្មួយ	niece or nephew

| ow-bpuk-kmeek | ឪពុកក្មេក | father-in-law |
| mdaay-kmeek | ម្ដាយក្មេក | mother-in-law |

aa-jiib អាជីព Occupations

look-gruu	លោកគ្រូ	teacher (male)
nek-gruu	អ្នកគ្រូ	teacher (female)
ni-set/goon-səh	និស្សិត/កូនសិស្ស	student
gruu-bpeet	គ្រូពេទ្យ	doctor
(gruu)-bpeet-tmeeñ	(គ្រូ)ពេទ្យធ្មេញ	dentist
mee-tia-vwii	មេធាវី	lawyer
nek-jəm-nuañ	អ្នកជំនួញ	businessman
nek-lok-doo	អ្នកលក់ដូរ	trader, businessman
nek-lok	អ្នកលក់	vendor
nek-tvwəə-srae	អ្នកធ្វើស្រែ	farmer
nek-nee-saat	អ្នកនេសាទ	fisherman
jiang	ជាង	skilled worker
jiang-chəə	ជាងឈើ	carpenter
jiang-maa-sin	ជាងម៉ាស៊ីន	mechanic
jiang-gat-dee	ជាងកាត់ដេរ	tailor, seamstress
jiang-gom-bpyuu-dtəə	ជាងកុំព្យូទ័រ	computer technician
nek-bɔɔk-bprae	អ្នកបកប្រែ	translator, interpreter
lee-kaa	លេខា	secretary
moo-dtoo-dob	ម៉ូតូឌុប	motorcycle taxi driver
mee-pdtɛah	មេផ្ទះ	housewife
jau-hvwaay	ចៅហ្វាយ	boss
nek-jat-gaa	អ្នកចាត់ការ	manager
oo-grit-ti-jon	ឧក្រិដ្ឋជន	criminal
bpoo-lih/dɔm-ruat	ប៉ូលិស / តម្រួត	police
bprɔɔ-tian	ប្រធាន	president
look-sɔɔng	លោកសង្ឃ	monk
dtua-aek-gon	តួឯកកុន	moviestar
dtɔm-naang-riah	តំណាងរាស្ត្រ	elected representative

nek-ni-bpon អ្នកនិពន្ធ author

sat សត្វ **Animals**

chmool ឈ្មោល male (for animals)
ñii ញី female (for animals)
chgae ឆ្កែ dog
chmaa ឆ្មា cat
dtrey ត្រី fish
jaab ចាប bird
dtao តោ lion
klaa ខ្លា tiger
klaa-kmum ខ្លាឃ្មុំ bear
dɔm-rey ដំរី elephant
moan មាន់ chicken
goo គោ cow, ox
jruuk ជ្រូក pig
seh សេះ horse
chluh ឈ្លូស deer
svwaa ស្វា monkey
bpoo-bpɛɛ ពពែ goat
jiam ចៀម sheep
chgae-jɔ-jɔɔk ឆ្កែចចក wolf
jiing-jɔk ជីងចក់ lizard
dtia ទា duck
grɔɔ-bey ក្របី water buffalo
grɔɔ-bpəə ក្រពើ crocodile
bpuah ពស់ snake
muuh មូស mosquito
ruy រុយ housefly
sii ស៊ី to eat (for animals)
ngoab ងាប់ to die (for animals)

Other Useful Words

dtii-grong	ទីក្រុង	city
srok-srae/jon-ɔ-bɔɔt	ស្រុកស្រែ/ជនបទ	countryside
bprɔ-lɔɔng	ប្រឡង	test, exam
aa-gia	អាគារ	building
gaa-ngia-tvəə	ការងារធ្វើ	job
daɯm-chəə	ដើមឈើ	tree
pgaa	ផ្កា	flower
pləəng	ភ្លើង	fire; electricity
ro-dteh-pləəng	រទេះភ្លើង	train
noo-yoo-baay	នយោបាយ	politics
see-ta-gek	សេដ្ឋកិច្ច	economy, economics
dtee-sɔ-jɔɔ	ទេសចរ	tourist
dtee-sɔ-jɔɔ	ទេសចរណ៍	tourism
gek-gaa	កិច្ចការ	matter; activity
gun-a-piab	គុណភាព	quality
dtuh-sa-naa-vwa-dey	ទស្សនាវដ្ដី	magazine
gom-bpyuu-dtəə	កុំព្យូទ័រ	computer
vwi-dtyu	វិទ្យុ	radio
dtuu	ទូ	cupboard/cabinet
dtuu-dtək-gɔɔk	ទូទឹកកក	refrigerator, freezer
doong	ដូង	coconut
tnaot	ត្នោត	palm fruit
grooik	ក្រូច	orange
bpaom	ប៉ោម	apple
svwaay	ស្វាយ	mango
jeek	ចេក	banana
saaw-maaw	សាវម៉ាវ	rambutan
saa-lat	សាឡាត់	lettuce
bpeeng-bpɔh	ប៉េងប៉ោះ	tomato
nom	នំ	cake; donut; baked goods; candy bars
nom-bpang	នំប៉័ង	bread

sgɔɔ-groab	ស្ករគ្រាប់	candy (pieces)
smau	ស្មៅ	grass
mlob	ម្លប់	shade
puum	ភូមិ	village
kaet	ខេត្ត	province
brɔ-jia-jon	ប្រជាជន	people
dɔm-nam	ដំណាំ	things you plant
grau	ក្រៅ	outside
gae	កែ	to correct
joab	ជាប់	to pass (a class or test)
tlɛak	ធ្លាក់	to fail (a class or test); to fall
bauk	បើក	to open, to turn on
bət	បិទ	to close, to turn off
rook-sii	រកស៊ី	to do business; make a living
dam	ដាំ	to plant, grow
kəəñ	ឃើញ	to see
dak	ដាក់	to place, put
jɔɔt	ចត	to park
ruah/ruah-nəu	រស់ / រស់នៅ	to live
nəu-ruah	នៅរស់	to be alive
rot	រត់	to run
bɔɔk-bprae	បកប្រែ	to translate, interpret
slab	ស្លាប់	to die
chob	ឈប់	to stop
choo	ឈរ	to stand
laung	ឡើង	to rise
choo laung	ឈរឡើង	to stand up
ɔng-guy	អង្គុយ	to sit
joh	ចុះ	to descend
ɔng-guy joh	អង្គុយចុះ	to sit down
gat	កាត់	to cut

"You"

There are many ways to correctly say "you" in Cambodian. We have previously learned only three of them: *nek, bɔɔng,* and *look.* Unfortunately, these three words cannot accurately represent even half of the instances to correctly convey the word "you." This next section will examine all the ways to say "you," including the ones previously discussed.

nek អ្នក		This is a generic word for "you." It is only used in conversation when speaking to someone younger or of a lower social status.
bɔɔng បង		This is used when speaking to someone older than yourself but younger than your parents. It can also be used when talking to a good friend who is close in age to yourself but may or may not be older.
bɔ-oon ប្អូន		This is used when speaking to someone younger than yourself but not young enough to be your child.
oon អូន		This is used when speaking to someone younger than yourself but not young enough to be your child. It can also be used by males when speaking to their lover.
kmuay ក្មួយ		This word means "niece" or "nephew" and is used when speaking to someone who is much younger than yourself (related or not) and young enough to be your child.
goon កូន		This word is used when speaking to your own children. It literally means "child."
bpaa ប៉ា		This is used when speaking to your father. It literally means "Dad."
maak/mae ម៉ាក់/ម៉ែ		This is used when speaking to your mother. It literally means "Mom."
bpuu ពូ		This means "uncle" and is used to address males (related or not) who are approximately as old as your father.

miing	មីង	This means "aunt" and is used to address females (related or not) who are approximately as old as your mother.
dtaa	តា	This means "grandfather" and is used to address males (related or not) who are approximately the age of your grandfather.
yiay	យាយ	This means "grandmother" and is used to address females (related or not) who are approximately the age of your grandmother.
om	អុំ	This is used when speaking to an older person regardless of gender. The person must be older than your parents.
look	លោក	This is used when speaking to someone of high status such as a monk, teacher, etc.
aek-oo-dtɔm	ឯកឧត្ដម	This is used when speaking to someone of very high social status such as a government minister. It literally means "your excellency."
bprɛah-ɔng	ព្រះអង្គ	This is used when speaking to either the king or God.

vwee-jia-gɔɔ   វេយ្យាករណ៍   **Grammar**

This chapter introduces few new gramatical concepts, but it does introduce important vocabulary. The family terms are very important and useful. When combined with the previously learned material, you can create many more new sentences as shown below.

> e.g. grua-saa kñom mian bpram nek. =
> There are five people in my family.
> kñom mian bɔ-oon-bproh bpii nek. =
> I have two younger brothers.
> knong grua-saa kñom, mian kñom, oo-bpuk-mdaay
> kñom, hauy-nəng bɔ-oon-bproh bpii nek. =
> In my family, there is me, my parents, and two
> younger brothers.

Another important section of this chapter is the section on occupations. Once again, when applied to previous material, you can create many new sentences.

> e.g. kñom jia gruu-bpeet. = I am a doctor.
> kñom rian kaang mee-tia-vwii. =
> I am studying to become a lawyer.

This chapter also introduces specific feelings. These feelings are expressed in the following manner.

> e.g. kñom bpi-baak-jet. = I am troubled.
> goat min səuw sɔb-baay-jet = He's not very happy.

The last and arguably most important part of this chapter is the section showing how to correctly say the word "you" in Cambodian. In Cambodian, people do not usually use a generic "you." Instead, they often call each other "uncle," "aunt," "grandpa," etc., even if they are not related. It is usually always based on age. Study this section very carefully, and use the appropriate word for each person you talk to.

__Conversation__

Sambo: | dtaʉ grua-saa ming mian bpon-maan nek dae?
សម្បួណ៌ | តើ ក្រុសារ មីង មាន ប៉ុន្មាន នាក់ ដែរ
How many people are in your family?

Kim: | grua-saa kñom mian bey nek: kñom, bdey kñom, haʉy-nəng goon-bproh mnek.
យិម | ក្រុសារ ខ្ញុំ មាន បី នាក់ ខ្ញុំ ប្ដី ខ្ញុំ
ហើយនិង កូនប្រុស ម្នាក់
There are three people in my family: myself, my husband, and my son.

Sambo: | ming min dtoan mian goon-srey dtee?
សម្បួណ៌ | មីង មិន ទាន់ មាន កូនស្រី ទេ
Don't you have any daughters yet?

Kim: | jaa. kñom min dtoan mian goon-srey nəʉ laʉy dtee. dtaʉ kmuay mian bɔɔng-bɔ-oon bpon-maan nek dae?
យិម | ចា៎ ខ្ញុំ មិន ទាន់ មាន កូនស្រី នៅ ឡើយ
ទេ តើ ក្មួយ មាន បងប្អូន
ប៉ុន្មាន នាក់ ដែរ
I do not have any daughters yet. How many brothers and sisters do you have?

Sambo: | kñom mian bɔɔng-bɔ-oon bey nek. mian bɔɔng-bproh bpii nek haʉy-nəng bɔ-oon-srey mnek.
សម្បួណ៌ | ខ្ញុំ មាន បងប្អូន បី នាក់ មាន
បងប្រុស ពីរ នាក់ ហើយនិង ប្អូនស្រី
ម្នាក់
I have three brothers and sisters. I have two older brothers and one younger sister.

klia ឃ្លា **Sentences**

1.   A: dtau goat riab-gaa hauy-ruu-nou?
     តើ គាត់ រៀបការ ហើយឬនៅ
     Is he married yet?

     B: nou, goat min dtoan gaa nou-lauy dtee.
     នៅ គាត់ មិន ទាន់ ការ នៅឡើយ ទេ
     No, he is still not married.

     C: baat, goat gaa hauy.
     បាទ គាត់ ការ ហើយ
     Yes, he's married.

     D: goat nou liiw.
     គាត់ នៅ លីវ
     He is still single.

2.   A: haet a-vwey bpuu ɔt tvwəə-gaa?
     ហេតុ អ្វី ពួ អត់ ធ្វើការ
     Why don't you work?

     B: bpii-bpruah kñom ɔh-gam-laang.
     ពីព្រោះ ខ្ញុំ អស់កម្លាំង
     Because I'm tired.

     C: bpii-bpruah kñom ngo-nguy-geeng.
     ពីព្រោះ ខ្ញុំ ងងុយគេង
     Because I'm sleepy.

     D: bpii-bpruah kñom bpi-baak-jet.
     ពីព្រោះ ខ្ញុំ ពិបាកចិត្ត
     Because I am sad.

     E: bpii-bpruah kñom mian sɔɔng-saa.
     ពីព្រោះ ខ្ញុំ មាន សង្សារ
     Because I have a girlfriend.

3.   A: dtaʉ look mian bɔɔng-bɔ-oon bpon-maan nek?
         តើ លោក មាន បងប្អូន ប៉ុន្មាន នាក់
         How many brothers and sisters do you have?

      B: kñom mian bɔɔng-bɔ-oon bpii nek: bɔɔng-bproh
         mnek nəng bɔ-oon-srey mnek.
         ខ្ញុំ មាន បងប្អូន ពីរ នាក់ បងប្រុស
         ម្នាក់ និង ប្អូនស្រី ម្នាក់
         I have two siblings: an older brother and a younger
         sister.

      C: kñom ɔt mian bɔɔng-bɔ-oon dtee.
         ខ្ញុំ អត់ មាន បងប្អូន ទេ
         I don't have any brothers and sisters.

4.   A: dtaʉ bpuu jool-jet mdaay-kmeek rʉʉ dtee?
         តើ ពូ ចូលចិត្ត ម្ដាយក្មេក ឬ ទេ
         Do you like your mother-in-law?

      B: kñom min jool-jet mdaay-kmeek kñom dtee.
         ខ្ញុំ មិន ចូលចិត្ត ម្ដាយក្មេក ខ្ញុំ ទេ
         I don't like my mother-in-law.

      C: baat, kñom jool-jet mdaay-kmeek kñom.
         បាទ ខ្ញុំ ចូលចិត្ត ម្ដាយក្មេក ខ្ញុំ
         Yes, I like my mother-in-law.

5.   A: dtaʉ ming jɔng tvwəə-gaa kaang ey dae?
         តើ មីង ចង់ ធ្វើការ ខាង អី ដែរ
         What kind of work do you want to do?

      B: kñom jɔng tvwəə-jia gruu-bpeet.
         ខ្ញុំ ចង់ ធ្វើជា គ្រូពេទ្យ
         I want to be a doctor.

      C: kñom jɔng tvwəə-jia dtua-aek-gon.
         ខ្ញុំ ចង់ ធ្វើជា តួឯកកុន
         I want to be a movie star.

D: kñom jɔng tvwəə-jia jiang-chəə.
ខ្ញុំ ចង់ ធ្វើជា ជាងឈើ
I want to be a carpenter.

6. A: goat rook-sii kaang naa dae?
គាត់ រកស៊ី ខាង ណា ដែរ
How does he earn a living?

B: goat bauk poo-ja-nii-taan kluan-aeng.
គាត់ បើក ភោជនីយដ្ឋាន ខ្លួនឯង
He opened his own restaurant.

C: goat jia nek-tvwəə-srae.
គាត់ ជា អ្នកធ្វើស្រែ
He is a farmer.

7. A: bprɔ-dteeh kmae mian sat a-vwey klah?
ប្រទេស ខ្មែរ មាន សត្វ អ្វី ខ្លះ
What animals are in Cambodia?

B: nəu bprɔ-dteeh kmae mian dɔm-rey jraun.
នៅ ប្រទេស ខ្មែរ មាន ដំរី ច្រើន
There are a lot of elephants in Cambodia.

C: bprɔ-dteeh kmae mian klaa hauy-nəng grɔɔ-bey.
ប្រទេស ខ្មែរ មាន ខ្លា ហើយនិង ក្របី
Cambodia has tigers and water buffalo.

D: bprɔ-dteeh kmae ɔt mian klaa-kmum dtee.
ប្រទេស ខ្មែរ អត់ មាន ខ្លាឃ្មុំ ទេ
There are no bears in Cambodia.

8. juay dak bpaom knong dtuu-dtək-gɔɔk baan dtee?
ជួយ ដាក់ ប៉ោម ក្នុង ទូទឹកកក បាន ទេ
Could you help put the apples in the refrigerator?

9. kñom jool-jet ɔng-guy graom mlob daum-chəə.
ខ្ញុំ ចូលចិត្ត អង្គុយ ក្រោម ម្លប់ ដើមឈើ
I enjoy sitting in the shade under the trees.

10. A: bɔɔng bprɔɔ-lɔɔng joab ruu dtee?
បង ប្រឡង ជាប់ ឬ ទេ
Did you pass the test?

B: baat, kñom joab.

បាទ ខ្ញុំ ជាប់

Yes, I passed.

C: kñom bprɔɔ-lɔɔng ɔt joab dtee.

ខ្ញុំ ប្រឡង អត់ ជាប់ ទេ

I did not pass the test.

D: dtee, kñom tlɛak.

ទេ ខ្ញុំ ធ្លាក់

No, I failed.

11. A: juay bauk dtuu-rə-dtuah baan dtee?[1]

ជួយ បើក ទូរទស្សន៍ បាន ទេ

Could you please turn on the television?

B: juay bət pləəng.[1]

ជួយ បិទ ភ្លើង

Please turn off the lights.

C: kñom soom bauk bɔɔng-uik baan dtee?

ខ្ញុំ សូម បើក បង្អួច បាន ទេ

May I open the window?

D: bət tvwia.

បិទ ទ្វារ

Shut the door.

12.   sat ɔt jeh sii nom-bpang dtee.

សត្វ អត់ ចេះ ស៊ី នំបុ័ង ទេ

Animals don't like to eat bread.

13.   kñom aan siaw-pəu jia bprɔɔ-jam.

ខ្ញុំ អាន សៀវភៅ ជា ប្រចាំ

I read books regularly.

14.   pdtɛah kñom mian ruy jraun nah.

ផ្ទះ ខ្ញុំ មាន រុយ ច្រើន ណាស់

My house has so many flies.

15.   kñom dam smau nəʉ kaang grau.

           ខ្ញុំ ដាំ ស្មៅ នៅ ខាង ក្រៅ

           I planted grass outside.

16.   A: yiay goat nəʉ-ruah dtee?

           យាយ គាត់ នៅរស់ ទេ

           Is his grandmother alive?

    B: yiay goat slab haʉy.

           យាយ គាត់ ស្លាប់ ហើយ

           His grandmother is dead.

    C: yiay goat nəʉ-ruah. goat nəʉ pnom-bpeeñ.

           យាយ គាត់ នៅរស់ គាត់ នៅ ភ្នំពេញ

           His grandmother is alive. She lives in Phnom Penh.

17.   A: dtaʉ look dtəʉ bpeet jia-muay nek naa?

           តើ លោក ទៅ ពេទ្យ ជាមួយ អ្នក ណា

           Who do you go to the doctor with?

    B: kñom dtəʉ bpeet mnek aeng.

           ខ្ញុំ ទៅ ពេទ្យ ម្នាក់ ឯង

           I go to the doctor by myself.

18.   A: dtaʉ goat dtəʉ gat smau jia-muay nek naa?

           តើ គាត់ ទៅ កាត់ ស្មៅ ជាមួយ អ្នក ណា

           Who does he go cut grass with?

    B: goat dtəʉ gat smau mnek-aeng.

           គាត់ ទៅ កាត់ ស្មៅ ម្នាក់ឯង

           He cuts the grass by himself.

19.   kñom bɔɔk-bprae daoy kluan-aeng.

           ខ្ញុំ បកប្រែ ដោយ ខ្លួនឯង

           I translated it by myself.

20.   bdey kñom gat sɔk kluan-aeng.

           ប្ដី ខ្ញុំ កាត់ សក់ ខ្លួនឯង

           My husband cuts his own hair.

21.   kñom jool-jet rian kmae daoy kluan-aeng.
             ខ្ញុំ   ចូលចិត្ត រៀន ខ្មែរ ដោយ   ខ្លួនឯង
             I enjoy studying Cambodian by myself.

22.   A: nih ro-bɔh nek naa?
           នេះ របស់   អ្នក ណា
           Whose is this?

      B: nih ro-bɔh kñom.
           នេះ របស់   ខ្ញុំ
           This is mine.

23.   aaw ro-bɔh kñom sa-aat nah.
             អាវ របស់   ខ្ញុំ   ស្អាត ណាស់
             My shirt is very pretty.

24.   A: ksae-dai nih jia ro-bɔh nek naa?
           ខ្សែដៃ នេះ ជា របស់   អ្នក ណា
           Whose bracelet is this?

      B: ksae-dai nih jia ro-bɔh kñom.
           ខ្សែដៃ នេះ ជា របស់   ខ្ញុំ
           This bracelet is mine.

      C: kñom min dəng taa ksae dai nih jia ro-bɔh nek naa
           dtee.
           ខ្ញុំ   មិន ដឹង ថា ខ្សែដៃ នេះ ជា របស់ អ្នក ណា
           ទេ
           I don't know who this bracelet belongs to.

      D: ksae-dai nih jia ro-bɔh goat, min mɛɛn jia ro-bɔh
           kñom dtee.
           ខ្សែដៃ នេះ ជា របស់   គាត់ មិន មែន ជា របស់
           ខ្ញុំ   ទេ
           This bracelet is hers, not mine.

Note: 1. In this context, the word *juay* (to help) is placed before a request
           suggesting that the speaker is asking another person to help do
           something for him. The use of *juay* in this manner is very
           common in spoken Cambodian.

Drills

1. Practice saying the following sentences in Cambodian. If the sentence is a question, practice answering it as well.

My girlfriend is heartbroken.

How many younger sisters do you have?

2. Do the following.

Describe your family in Cambodian. You must tell how many family members you have and identify each member.

Tell what occupation you currently do (or would like to do) and give at least one reason why you like it.

3. Use the following words to help form ten sentences.

kñom	chgae	tvwəə-jia
jɔng	sgoal	jih
muay	jbab	choo-laung
look-sɔɔng	soom	goat
min	mian	nek
oo-grit-ti-jon	dtoan	jia
ñam	krooik	dtəu
mnek-aeng	nəu-lauy	dtee
jiang	bpaom	jool-jet
juab	maong	tloab
muay	dtau	saa-lat

Test 10

Match the English words with the Cambodian words.

_____ 1. mother   a. doong   ដូង

_____ 2. confused   b. jruuk   ជ្រូក

_____ 3. building   c. bdey   ប្ដី

_____ 4. radio   d. gruu-bpeet   គ្រូពេទ្យ

_____ 5. coconut   e. jrɔ-lɔɔm   ច្រឡំ

_____ 6. to see   f. ni-set   និស្សិត

_____ 7. pig   g. ngo-nguy-deek   ងងុយដេក

_____ 8. to sit   h. vwi-dtyu   វិទ្យុ

_____ 9. cabinet   i. bpeet-tmeeñ   ពេទ្យធ្មេញ

_____ 10. to live   j. goo   គោ

_____ 11. husband   k. liiw   លីវ

_____ 12. single   l. ɔng-guy   អង្គុយ

_____ 13. sleepy   m. mdtaay   ម្ដាយ

_____ 14. to correct   n. kəəñ   ឃើញ

_____ 15. student   o. dtuu   ទូ

_____ 16. dentist   p. gae   កែ

                                      q. aa-gia   អាគារ

                                      r. ruah   រស់

Several types of people are listed below. Write the appropriate word you would use for "you" when speaking to these people.

1. A woman twenty years older than you   _____

2. An old man older than your parents   _____

3. A person five years younger than you   _____

4. A person twenty years younger than you   _____

5. The king   _____

6. A person your age   _____

7. A government minister   _____

8. Your boss   _____

9. A good friend   _____

10. Any old person older than your parents   _____

11. Your grandmother   _____

12. Your father   _____

13. A monk   _____

14. Your younger brother   _____

15. A man twenty years older than you   _____

Reading Exercise

Read and translate the following sentences into English.

1. ខ្ញុំ មិន សួរ សប្បាយចិត្ត ទេ ។

2. តើ បង ចង់ ញ៉ាំ មូប ប៉ុន្មាន ចាន ដែរ?

3. អាគារ នេះ មាន ប៉ុន្មាន ជាន់?

4. ផ្កា មិន អាច ដុះ នៅ លើ ថ្ម បាន ទេ ។

5. ខ្ញុំ ចូលចិត្ត មូប ខ្មែរ និង មូប ថៃ ប៉ុន្តែ មូប ចិន ប្រៃ ពេក ។

6. ពូ ខ្ញុំ មិន ដែល រៀន ភាសា អង់គ្លេស ទេ ។

7. ខ្ញុំ ស្គាល់ និស្សិត ប្រាំ នាក់ ។

8. គាត់ រៀន ខាង សេដ្ឋកិច្ច ។

9. បង ខ្ញុំ បាន ទៅ លេង ប្រទេស ចិន ហើយនិង ប្រទេស ជប៉ុន ។

10. ឪពុកម្ដាយ ខ្ញុំ ធ្វើការ ក្នុង ភោជនីយដ្ឋាន ។

11. ខ្ញុំ ហើយនិង តា ខ្ញុំ និង ជួប គ្នា នៅ ម៉ោង ប្រាំមួយ ព្រឹក ។

12. ស្រុកអាមេរិក មិន ដូច ស្រុកខ្មែរ ទេ ។

13. ឪពុក ខ្ញុំ មក ពី ភ្នំពេញ ប៉ុន្តែ ម្ដាយ ខ្ញុំ មក ពី បាត់ដំបង ។

14. គាត់ ចង់ ធ្វើការ ប៉ុន្តែ រក ការងារធ្វើ មិន បាន ។

15. បើ អ្នក ចង់ ចេះ ភាសា ខ្មែរ ត្រូវ រៀន ប្រចាំ ថ្ងៃ ។

16. មាន ទេសចរ ច្រើន នាក់ មក ស្រុកខ្មែរ ប្រចាំ ឆ្នាំ ។

17. តើ បង ចង់ ទៅ មើល កុន ឬ ចង់ ទៅ រត់លេង?

18. ខ្ញុំ ចង់ លេង បាល់ ប៉ុន្តែ ខ្ញុំ លេង មិន បាន ទេ ព្រោះ ខ្ញុំ ឈឺ
    ខ្លាំង ។

19. គាត់ រកស៊ី ជា អ្នកនេសាទ ព្រោះ គាត់ មិន បាន រៀន ចប់
    សាកលវិទ្យាល័យ ទេ ។

20. ធម្មតា ខ្ញុំ ធ្វើការ ពី ម៉ោង ប្រាំបី ព្រឹក រហូត ដល់ ម៉ោង ប្រាំមួយ
    ល្ងាច ប៉ុន្តែ ខ្ញុំ អត់ ធ្វើការ នៅ ថ្ងៃ សុក្រ ទេ ។

21. ប្រទេសខ្មែរ នៅ កណ្តាល ប្រទេស ថៃ និង ប្រទេស
    វៀតណាម ។

22. ខ្ញុំ ស្គាល់ បងប្អូន គាត់ ពីរ នាក់ ប៉ុន្តែ ខ្ញុំ មិន ស្គាល់ ឪពុកម្តាយ
    គាត់ ទេ ។

23. តើ សត្វ គោ មាន ជើង ប៉ុន្មាន ដែរ?

24. ឡាន គាត់ ថ្មី ប៉ុន្តែ វា ខូច ច្រើន ។

25 ខ្ញុំ មិន ចង់ ទៅ ទីក្រុង ពីព្រោះ អត់ មាន កន្លែង ចត ឡាន ទេ ។

26. យន្តហោះ លឿន ជាង រទេះភ្លើង ។

27. ដើរលេង នៅ ជនបទ សប្បាយ ជាង ដើរលេង នៅ ទីក្រុង ។

28. ប្រទេសខ្មែរ ចាស់ ជាង ប្រទេស អាមេរិក ប៉ុន្តែ ប្រទេស ចិន ចាស់ ជាង ប្រទេស ខ្មែរ ។

29. សាលា នេះ មាន កូនសិស្ស ៣០០ នាក់ ។

30. អក្សរ ខ្មែរ មិន ស្រួល អាន ទេ ។

31. ខ្ញុំ នៅ ជាមួយ ម្ដាយក្មេក ព្រោះ ខ្ញុំ មិន សូវ មាន លុយ ទេ ។

32. ឡាន នេះ ក៏ លឿន ដែរ ។

Read the following paragraphs and translate. In these paragraphs, words will not be separated by spaces. Some of these passages use a few words that have not yet been introduced in this book. Those words and their definitions are listed at the bottom of the next page.

ប្រជាជនខ្មែរភាគច្រើនជាអ្នកធ្វើស្រែ ។ នៅស្រុកខ្មែរ អ្នកធ្វើស្រែដាំដំណាំ ច្រើនយ៉ាង ប៉ុន្តែ ធម្មតាដាំតែស្រូវទេ ។ ស្រូវរស់ខាន់ណាស់ពីព្រោះ ប្រជាជនខ្មែរចូលចិត្តញ៉ាំបាយ ប៉ុន្តែអ្នកធ្វើស្រែ ដាំបន្លែនិងផ្លែឈើដែរ ។ ប្រជាជនខ្មែរចូលចិត្តផ្លែឈើណាស់ ។ ពួកគេចូលចិត្តញ៉ាំផ្លែឈើដូចជា ស្វាយ សាវម៉ាវ និងក្រូច ។

គ្រួសារខ្ញុំមកពីជនបទ ប៉ុន្តែខ្ញុំបានមកនៅទីក្រុងភ្នំពេញហើយ ។ ខ្ញុំមក ភ្នំពេញដើម្បីចូលរៀននៅសាកលវិទ្យាល័យ ។ ខ្ញុំចង់រៀនខាងពេទ្យដើម្បី អាចធ្វើជាគ្រូពេទ្យបាន ។ ខ្ញុំមិនចង់ធ្វើជាអ្នកធ្វើស្រែដូចជាឪពុកម្ដាយខ្ញុំ ទេ ។ កិច្ចការធ្វើស្រែពិបាកណាស់ ហើយអ្នកធ្វើស្រែក្រដែរ ។ ខ្ញុំគិតថា នៅទីក្រុងល្អជាងនៅជនបទ ។

នៅក្នុងភូមិខ្ញុំមានជនជាតិខ្មែរច្រើននាក់ ប៉ុន្តែមានជនជាតិភាគតិចខ្លះដែរ ។
មានជនជាតិវៀតណាមខ្លះ ហើយមានជនជាតិលាវខ្លះ ប៉ុន្តែពួកគេបាន
រៀនចេះភាសាខ្មែរយើងហើយ ។

ខ្ញុំជាអ្នកលក់សំឡេ។រកបំពាក់នៅផ្សារថ្មីនៅទីក្រុងភ្នំពេញ ។ សំឡេ។រកបំពាក់
ខ្ញុំមានច្រើនយ៉ាង ។ ខ្ញុំមានសំឡេ។រកបំពាក់អាមេរិកាំង ហើយមាន
សំឡេ។រកបំពាក់ខ្មែរដែរ ។ ធម្មតាខ្ញុំបើកហាងនៅម៉ោងប្រាំមួយព្រឹក ហើយ
បិទហាងនៅម៉ោងប្រាំល្ងាច ។ មានទេសចរច្រើននាក់មកទិញ
សំឡេ។រកបំពាក់ខ្ញុំ ។ ពួកគេនិយាយថា សំឡេ។រកបំពាក់ខ្ញុំថោក ស្អាត ហើយ
មានគុណភាពល្អ ។ ពេលខ្លះគេទិញសំឡេ។រកបំពាក់សំរាប់បងប្អូននិង
ពួកម៉ាកគេដែរ ។ ប្រជាជនខ្មែរមកទិញសំឡេ។រកបំពាក់ខ្ញុំដែរ ប៉ុន្តែពួកគេ
មិនសូវទិញច្រើនដូចពួកទេសចរទេ ។

Extra Vocabulary

srəɨw	ស្រូវ	unmilled rice
jun-jiat	ជនជាតិ	nationality, citizenship
liaw	លាវ	Lao, Laotian
psaa-tmey	ផ្សារថ្មី	the largest market in Phnom Penh

Appendix I
Useful Words and Phrases

General Conversation

Hello.	jəm-riab-sua. ជំរាបសួរ
Goodbye.	jəm-riab-lia / lia-haʉy / lia-sen-haʉy ជំរាបលា / លាហើយ / លាសិនហើយ
Good day.	sua-sdey. សួស្ដី
Good morning.	a-run sua-sdey. អរុនសួស្ដី
Good night.	ria-dtrey sua-sdey. រាត្រីសួស្ដី
How are you doing?	sok-sɔb-baay dtee? សុខសប្បាយទេ
How's it going?	yaang meeik dae? យ៉ាងមេ៉ចដែរ
Fine.	sok-sɔb-baay. សុខសប្បាយ
Not so good.	min-səʉw-sɔb-baay dtee មិនសូវសប្បាយទេ
I don't feel very well.	kñom min səʉw srual kluan dtee. ខ្ញុំមិនសូវស្រួលខ្លួនទេ
I'm sick.	kñom chʉʉ. ខ្ញុំឈឺ
So-so.	tom-mdaa ធម្មតា
See you later.	juab knia tgnai graoy dtiat. ជួបគ្នាថ្ងៃក្រោយទៀត
See you tomorrow.	juab knia (tngai) sa-aek (dtiat). ជួបគ្នា(ថ្ងៃ)ស្អែក(ទៀត)
Take care. Have a good one.	sok-sɔb-baay dtaam pləʉw. សុខសប្បាយតាមផ្លូវ

Pleased to meet you.	kñom sɔb-baay-jet baan juab look. ខ្ញុំសប្បាយចិត្តបានជួបលោក
Thank you very much.	ɔɔ-gun jraɥn. អរគុណច្រើន
I'm sorry.	soom dtooh. សូមទោស
Excuse me.	ɔt dtooh. អត់ទោស
Long time no see.	bat mok bat moat. បាត់មុខបាត់មាត់
Who?	nek naa? អ្នកណា
What?	sa-ey? / a-vwey? / ey? ស្ដី / អ្វី / អី
Where?	nəɥ naa/nəɥ (ae) naa? នៅណា / នៅ(ឯ)ណា
When?	ɔng-gaal? / bpii-ɔng-gaal? អង្កាល / ពីអង្កាល
Why?	haet-ey? / haet a-vwey? ហេតុអី / ហេតុអ្វី
How?	yaang-naa? យ៉ាងណា
Whose?	ro-bɔh nek naa? របស់អ្នកណា
What do you want to do?	jɔng tvwəə ey klah dae? ចង់ធ្វើអីខ្លះដែរ
Where is the bathroom?	bɔn-dtub-dtək nəɥ ae naa? បន្ទប់ទឹកនៅឯណា
market?	psaa ផ្សារ
hotel?	sɔɔn-taa-gia / oo-dtael សណ្ឋាគារ / អូតែល
hospital?	mon-dtii-bpeet មន្ទីរពេទ្យ
airport?	vwial-yun-hɔh វាលយន្តហោះ

embassy?	staan-dtuut	ស្ថានទូត
What's this?	sa-ey nih?	ស្អីនេះ
This	aa-nih	អានេះ
What's that?	sa-ey nuh?	ស្អីនោះ
That	aa-nuh/aa-nəng	អានោះ / ហ្នឹង
Here	dtii-nih	ទីនេះ
There	dtii-nuh	ទីនោះ
Over there.	nuh-nɔɔ.	នោះហ្នុ
Whose is this?	nih ro-bɔh nek naa? នេះរបស់អ្នកណា	
How much?	tlai bpon-maan?	ថ្លៃប៉ុន្មាន
How much is this?	aa-nih tlai bpon-maan? អានេះថ្លៃប៉ុន្មាន	
Hello? (on the phone)	aa-loo?	អាឡោ
Is John home.	dtaʉ jɔɔn nəʉ pdtɛah dtee? តើចននៅផ្ទះទេ	
I would like to speak with John.	kñom jɔng ni-yiay jia-muay jɔɔn. ខ្ញុំចង់និយាយជាមួយចន	
John is not home.	jɔɔn ɔt nəʉ pdtɛah dtee. ចនអត់នៅផ្ទះទេ	
Really?	mɛɛn? / an-jəng?	មែន / អញ្ចឹង
Right?	mɛɛn dtee?	មែនទេ
If	baʉ	បើ
Because	bpruah / bpii-bpruah ព្រោះ / ពីព្រោះ	
Not yet.	min dtoan dtee.	មិនទាន់ទេ

Already finished.	haɨy-haɨy.	ហើយៗ
But	bpon-dtae	ប៉ុន្តែ
Don't.	gom.	កុំ
Don't do it.	gom tvwəə.	កុំធ្វើ
Don't go.	gom dtəɨ.	កុំទៅ
Maybe	bprɔɔ-hael	ប្រហែល
Please	soom / som	សូម / សុំ
Where are you going?	dtəɨ naa?	ទៅណា
Have you eaten?	ñam baay haɨy rɨɨ nəɨ?	ញុំាបាយហើយឬនៅ
What's your name?	dtaɨ look chmuah ey?	តើលោកឈ្មោះអី
My name is John.	kñom chmuah jɔɔn.	ខ្ញុំឈ្មោះចន
What kind of work do you do?	dtaɨ look tvwəə-gaa kaang ey dae?[1]	តើលោកធ្វើការខាងអីដែរ
I'm a doctor.	kñom jia gruu-bpeet.	ខ្ញុំជាគ្រូពេទ្យ
lawyer	mee-tia-vwii	មេធាវី
student	ni-set / goon-səh	និស្សិត / កូនសិស្ស
professor	sah-straa-jaa	សាស្ត្រាចារ្យ
diplomat	nek-gaa-dtuut	អ្នកការទូត
tourist	dtee-sɔ-jɔɔ	ទេសចរ
Where are you from?	dtaɨ look mook bpii naa?	តើលោកមកពីណា

I'm from America.	kñom mook bpii srok aa-mee-rik.[2] ខ្ញុំមកពីស្រុកអាមេរិក
France	srok baa-rang ស្រុកបារាំង
Australia	srok oo-straa-lii ស្រុកអូស្ត្រាលី
China	srok jen ស្រុកចិន
Thailand	srok tai ស្រុកថៃ
Vietnam	srok vwiat-naam ស្រុកវៀតណាម
Do you like Cambodia?	dtaʉ look jool-jet srok-kmae dtee? តើលោកចូលចិត្តស្រុកខ្មែរទេ
The Cambodian people are very nice.	bprɔ-jia-jon kmae lɔ-ɔɔ nah. ប្រជាជនខ្មែរល្អណាស់
Cambodia is very hot.	srok kmae gdau nah. ស្រុកខ្មែរក្តៅណាស់
Cambodia is very beautiful.	srok kmae sa-aat nah. ស្រុកខ្មែរស្អាតណាស់
It rains a lot.	pliang jraʉn nah. ភ្លៀងច្រើនណាស់
Cambodia is a tough place to live.	srok kmae bpi-baak nəʉ. ស្រុកខ្មែរពិបាកនៅ
Cambodia is an easy place to live.	srok kmae srual nəʉ. ស្រុកខ្មែរស្រួលនៅ
I like Phnom Penh.	kñom jool-jet pnom bpeeñ. ខ្ញុំចូលចិត្តភ្នំពេញ
Can you speak Cambodian?	dtaʉ look jeh ni-yiay pia-saa kmae dtee? តើលោកចេះនិយាយភាសាខ្មែរទេ

Can you speak English?

dtau look jeh ni-yiay pia-saa ɔng-glee dtee?
តើលោកចេះនិយាយភាសាអង់គ្លេសទេ

I speak a little Cambodian.

kñom jeh ni-yiay pia-saa kmae bɔn-dtek-bɔn-dtuuik.
ខ្ញុំចេះនិយាយភាសាខ្មែរបន្តិចបន្តួច

Please speak slowly.

soom ni-yiay muay muay.
សូមនិយាយមួយៗ

Please say that again.

soom taa mdɔɔng dtiat.
សូមថាម្តងទៀត

Can you write Cambodian script?

jeh sɔɔ-see ak-sɔɔ kmae dtee? ចេះសរសេរអក្សរខ្មែរទេ

I can write a little Cambodian script.

kñom jeh sɔɔ-see ak-sɔɔ kmae bɔn-dtek-bɔn-dtuuik.
ខ្ញុំចេះសរសេរអក្សរខ្មែរបន្តិចបន្តួច

I don't understand.

kñom sdab min baan.
ខ្ញុំស្តាប់មិនបាន

I can't hear.

kñom sdab min lɯɯ.
ខ្ញុំស្តាប់មិនឮ

I am studying Cambodian.

kñom gɔm-bpung rian pia-saa kmae.
ខ្ញុំកំពុងរៀនភាសាខ្មែរ

I am learning Cambodian from this book.

kñom rian pia-saa kmae bpii siaw-pɯu nih.
ខ្ញុំរៀនភាសាខ្មែរពីសៀវភៅនេះ

How do you say this in Cambodian?

nih kmae taa meeik?
នេះខ្មែរថាម៉េច

What does ____ mean?

____ mian ney taa meeik?
____ មានន័យថាម៉េច

How old are you?	dtaʉ look aa-yu bpon-maan haʉy? តើលោកអាយុប៉ុន្មានហើយ
I'm thirty years old.	kñom aa-yu saam-seb chnam. ខ្ញុំអាយុសាមសិបឆ្នាំ
Where do you live?	dtaʉ look nəʉ ae naa dae? តើលោកនៅឯណាដែរ
I live at (in) _____.	kñom nəʉ _____. ខ្ញុំនៅ _____.
How many brothers and sisters do you have?	dtaʉ look mian bɔɔng-bɔ-oon bpon-maan nek? តើលោកមានបងប្អូនប៉ុន្មាននាក់
Are you married?	dtaʉ nek riab-gaa haʉy rʉʉ nəʉ? តើអ្នករៀបការហើយឬនៅ
I'm married.	kñom riab-gaa haʉy. ខ្ញុំរៀបការហើយ
I'm single.	kñom nəʉ liiw. ខ្ញុំនៅលីវ
I'm divorced.	kñom lɛɛng knia haʉy. ខ្ញុំលែងគ្នាហើយ
My wife passed away.	brɔɔ-bpon kñom slab haʉy. ប្រពន្ធខ្ញុំស្លាប់ហើយ
How is the weather?	tiat-aa-gah yaang meeik dae? ធាតុអាកាសយ៉ាងម៉េចដែរ
It's hot.	gdau. ក្តៅ
It's cold.	dtrɔ-jɛak. ត្រជាក់
Can I see you tomorrow?	juab knia sa-aek baan dtee? ជួបគ្នាស្អែកបានទេ

Can you teach me Cambodian?	juay bɔng-rian kñom pia-saa kmae baan dtee? ជួយបង្រៀនខ្ញុំភាសាខ្មែរបានទេ
I like _____.	kñom jool-jet _____. ខ្ញុំចូលចិត្ត _____.
I don't like _____.	kñom min jool-jet _____. ខ្ញុំមិនចូលចិត្ត _____.
I like Cambodian people.	kñom jool-jet bɔɔng-ba-oon kmae. ខ្ញុំចូលចិត្តបងប្អូនខ្មែរ
You are kind.	look mian jet lɔ-ɔɔ nah. លោកមានចិត្តល្អណាស់
Where are you staying?	dtaʉ look snak nəʉ ae naa? តើលោកស្នាក់នៅឯណា
I am staying at the Royal Hotel.	kñom snak nəʉ sɔn-taa-gia roo-yaal. ខ្ញុំស្នាក់នៅសណ្ឋាគាររ៉ូយ៉ាល
Here is my address.	nih jia aa-saay-a-taan ro-bɔh kñom. នេះជាអាស័យដ្ឋានរបស់ខ្ញុំ
Here is my phone number.	nih jia leek dtuu-re-sab ro-bɔh kñom. នេះជាលេខទូរស័ព្ទរបស់ខ្ញុំ
Can I have your address?	kñom som aa-saay-a-taan ro-bɔh look baan dtee? ខ្ញុំសុំអាស័យដ្ឋានរបស់លោកបានទេ
Can I have your phone number?	kñom som leek dtuu-re-sab ro-bɔh look baan dtee? ខ្ញុំសុំលេខទូរស័ព្ទរបស់លោកបានទេ
Give me a call.	soom añ-jəəñ dtuu-re-sab mook kñom. សូមអញ្ជើញទូរស័ព្ទមកខ្ញុំ

Can I give you a call?	kñom soom dtuu-re-sab dtəu look baan dtee? ខ្ញុំសូមទូរស័ព្ទទៅលោកបានទេ
I'm leaving tomorrow.	kñom jeeñ dtəu sa-aek. ខ្ញុំចេញទៅស្អែក
I'm going back to my country next week.	aa-dtit graoy kñom trɔ-lɔb dtəu srok kñom vwiñ. អាទិត្យក្រោយខ្ញុំត្រឡប់ទៅស្រុកខ្ញុំវិញ

Note: 1. The word "you" is represented in these examples by the word
            look. When you actually say these phrases, be sure to use
            the correct word for "you" depending on who you're
            speaking to as shown in Chapter 10.
        2. The word "country" is represented in these phrases by the word
            srok. However, be sure to use another word such as
            brɔ-dteeh if the situation is more formal

In a Restaurant

I want to order _____.	kñom jɔng yook _____. ខ្ញុំចង់យក _____.
What would you like to eat?	jɔng ñam ey klah dae? ចង់ញាំអ៊ីខ្លះដែរ
What would you like to drink?	jɔng ñam dtək ey dae? ចង់ញាំទឹកអ៊ីដែរ
May I have some water?	som dtək-sot baan dtee? សុំទឹកសុទ្ធបានទេ
I would like one serving of fried rice.	kñom jɔng yook baay chaa muay jaan. ខ្ញុំចង់យកបាយឆាមួយចាន
I would like some more rice.	som baay taem. សុំបាយថែម
May I have some ice?	som dtək-gɔɔk baan dtee? សុំទឹកកកបានទេ
Is it spicy?	həl dtee? ហឹរទេ
Is it too spicy?	həl bpeek dtee? ហឹរពេកទេ
It's very spicy.	həl nah. ហឹរណាស់
It's not spicy.	min həl dtee. មិនហឹរទេ
Does it taste good?	chngañ dtee? ឆ្ងាញ់ទេ
It's delicious.	chngañ. ឆ្ងាញ់
This food is very delicious.	mhoob nih chngañ nah. ម្ហូបនេះឆ្ងាញ់ណាស់
It doesn't taste good.	min chngañ dtee. មិនឆ្ងាញ់ទេ
I like to eat Cambodian food.	kñom jool-jet ñam mhoob kmae. ខ្ញុំចូលចិត្តញាំម្ហូបខ្មែរ

I want dessert.	kñom jɔng baan bɔng-aem. ខ្ញុំចង់បានបង្អែម
I'm full.	kñom cha-aet hauy. ខ្ញុំឆ្អែតហើយ
That's enough.	baan hauy. បានហើយ
I'm drunk.	kñom srɔ-vwəng hauy. ខ្ញុំស្រវឹងហើយ
alcohol	sraa ស្រា
Cambodian food	mhoob kmae ម្ហូបខ្មែរ
Can I have the bill?	git luy. គិតលុយ
beef	saik-goo សាច់គោ
beer	bia បៀរ
boil/boiled	sngao ស្ងោរ
chicken	saik-moan សាច់មាន់
coffee	gaa-hvwee កាហ្វេ
crab	gdtaam ក្ដាម
curry	gaa-rii ការី
dessert	bɔng-aem បង្អែម
delicious	chngañ ឆ្ងាញ់
duck	dtia ទា
eat	ñam ញ៉ាំ
egg	bpoong ពង
egg noodles	mii មី
fish	dtrey ត្រី
food	mhoob ម្ហូប
fry/fried	chaa ឆា

fruit	plae-chəə	ផ្លែឈើ
grill/grilled	ang	អាំង
ice	dtək-gɔɔk	ទឹកកក
milk	dtək-dɔh-goo	ទឹកដោះគោ
pork	saik-jruuk	សាច់ជ្រូក
porridge	bɔ-bɔɔ	បបរ
rice (cooked)	baay	បាយ
rice noodles	guy-dtiaw	កុយទាវ
seafood	mhoob grɨang sa-mot	ម្ហូបគ្រឿងសមុទ្រ
shrimp	bɔng-gia	បង្គា
soup	sɔm-lɔɔ/sub	សម្ល / ស៊ុប
tea	dtae	តែ
vegetable	bɔn-lae	បន្លែ
vegetarian	mo-nuh dtɔɔm saik	មនុស្សតមសាច់

Expressing Needs and Feelings

I'm hungry.	kñom klian baay. ខ្ញុំឃ្លានបាយ
I'm thirsty.	kñom sreek dtək. ខ្ញុំស្រេកទឹក
I'm tired/exhausted.	kñom ɔh gam-lang. ខ្ញុំអស់កម្លាំង
I'm sleepy.	kñom ngo-nguay deek. ខ្ញុំងងុយដេក
I'm happy.	kñom sɔb-baay-jet. ខ្ញុំសប្បាយចិត្ត
I'm excited.	kñom rəm-pəəb jet. ខ្ញុំរំភើបចិត្ត
I'm hot.	kñom gdau. ខ្ញុំក្តៅ
I'm cold.	kñom dtrɔ-jɛak. ខ្ញុំត្រជាក់
I don't feel very well.	kñom min səɰw srual kluan. ខ្ញុំមិនសូវស្រួលខ្លួន
I'm sick.	knom chɰɰ. ខ្ញុំឈឺ
I have a headache.	kñom chɰɰ gbaal. ខ្ញុំឈឺក្បាល
I have a stomachache.	kñom chɰɰ bpuah. ខ្ញុំឈឺពោះ
I need some medicine.	kñom dtrəɰw ñam tnam. ខ្ញុំត្រូវញ៉ាំថ្នាំ
I need some sleep.	kñom dtrəɰw deek. ខ្ញុំត្រូវដេក
I want to see a doctor.	kñom jɔng juab gruu-bpeet. ខ្ញុំចង់ជួបគ្រូពេទ្យ
Come here.	mook nih. មកនេះ

Help!	juay kñom pɔɔng! ជួយខ្ញុំផង
Watch out!	bprɔ-yat! ប្រយ័ត្ន
I want to drink some water.	kñom jɔng ñam dtək-sot. ខ្ញុំចង់ញ៉ាំទឹកសុទ្ធ
I want to have a glass of beer.	kñom jɔng ñam bia muay gaew. ខ្ញុំចង់ញ៉ាំបៀរមួយកែវ
I want to buy some medicine.	kñom jɔng dtiñ tnam. ខ្ញុំចង់ទិញថ្នាំ
I want to use the restroom.	kñom jɔng bprau bon-dtub-dtək. ខ្ញុំចង់ប្រើបន្ទប់ទឹក
It's too loud.	tlɔng bpeek. ថ្លង់ពេក
Can you turn down the air conditioner?	juay bon-tɔɔy maa-sin dtrɔ-jeak bon-dtek baan dtee? ជួយបន្ទយម៉ាស៊ីនត្រជាក់បន្ថិចបានទេ
Can you turn up the air conditioner?	juay bauk maa-sin dtrɔ-jeak aoy klang bon-dtek baan dtee? ជួយបើកម៉ាស៊ីនត្រជាក់ឱ្យខ្លាំងបន្ថិច បានទេ
Can you turn on the fan?	juay bauk dɔng-hal baan dtee? ជួយបើកដង្ហាល់បានទេ
May I use the telephone?	kñom soom bprau dtuu-re-sab baan dtee? ខ្ញុំសូមប្រើទូរស័ព្ទបានទេ
May I have some more water?	som dtək-sot taem baan dtee? សុំទឹកសុទ្ធថែមបានទេ
I'm lost.	kñom vwoong-vweeng hauy. ខ្ញុំវង្វេងហើយ

How do I get to _____?	pləɰ naa noam dtəɰ ផ្លូវណានាំទៅ _____?
I need more money.	kñom dtrəɰw-gaa luy taem. ខ្ញុំត្រូវការលុយថែម
I need to go to the bank.	kñom dtrəɰw dtəɰ to-nia-gia. ខ្ញុំត្រូវទៅធនាគារ
I need to exchange money.	kñom dtrəɰw doo luy. ខ្ញុំត្រូវដូរលុយ
I want to go home.	kñom jɔng dtrɔ-lɔb dtəɰ pdtɛah vwiñ. ខ្ញុំចង់ត្រឡប់ទៅផ្ទះវិញ
I want to _____ (verb).	kñom jɔng _____. ខ្ញុំចង់ _____.
I want _____ (noun).	kñom jɔng baan _____. ខ្ញុំចង់បាន _____.
I understand.	kñom yul. ខ្ញុំយល់
I don't understand.	kñom min yul dtee. ខ្ញុំមិនយល់ទេ
I don't know.	kñom min dəng dtee. ខ្ញុំមិនដឹងទេ
I think so too. / I agree.	kñom git an-jəng dae. ខ្ញុំគិតអញ្ចឹងដែរ
I believe (you).	kñom jɰa. ខ្ញុំជឿ
I don't believe (you).	kñom min jɰa dtee. ខ្ញុំមិនជឿទេ
I'm sure.	kñom dəng jbah. ខ្ញុំដឹងច្បាស់
I'm not sure.	kñom min dtiang dtee. ខ្ញុំមិនទៀងទេ
I'm joking.	kñom taa leeng. ខ្ញុំថាលេង

No problem.	ɔt mian bɔñ-ña-haa dtee. អត់មានបញ្ហាទេ
A little bit	bɔn-dtek-bɔn-dtuuik បន្តិចបន្តួច
I forgot.	kñom pleek. ខ្ញុំភ្លេច
I don't remember.	kñom jam min baan. ខ្ញុំចាំមិនបាន
Let's go.	dɔh dtəʉ. ដោះទៅ
I'm busy.	kñom ro-vwul. ខ្ញុំរវល់
I'm happy.	kñom sɔb-baay-jet. ខ្ញុំសប្បាយចិត្ត
I'm sad.	kñom bpi-baak-jet. ខ្ញុំពិបាកចិត្ត
I'm angry.	kñom kəng. ខ្ញុំខឹង
I'm mad at myself.	kñom kəng kluan aeng. ខ្ញុំខឹងខ្លួនឯង
I'm homesick.	kñom nək srok. ខ្ញុំនឹកស្រុក
I'm confused.	kñom jrɔ-lɔm. ខ្ញុំច្រឡំ
I'm embarrassed.	kñom kmah gee. ខ្ញុំខ្មាសគេ
I'm bored.	kñom ɔb-sok. ខ្ញុំអផ្សុក
I'm worried.	kñom bpruay-baa-rom. ខ្ញុំព្រួយបារម្ភ
I'm scared.	kñom klaaik. ខ្ញុំខ្លាច
I'm hurt (emotionally).	kñom kooik-jet. ខ្ញុំខូចចិត្ត
No smoking.	haam jok baa-rey. ហាមជក់បារី

Speak up.

soom ni-yiay klang klang.
សូមនិយាយខ្លាំងៗ

I made a mistake.

kñom baan tvwəə koh.
ខ្ញុំបានធ្វើខុស

Wait a minute.

soom jam muay plɛɛt.
សូមចាំមួយភ្លែត

Happy Birthday.

sua-sdey tngai gɔm-naut.
សួស្ដីថ្ងៃកំណើត

Merry Christmas.

sua-sdey bon noo-ael.
សួស្ដីបុណ្យណូអែល

Good luck.

soom aoy mian sɔm-naang
lɔ-ɔɔ.　សូមឱ្យមានសំណាងល្អ

I wish you happiness.

soom aoy baan
sek-gdey-sok.
សូមឱ្យបានសេចក្ដីសុខ

Happy New Year.

sua-sdey chnam tmey.
សួស្ដីឆ្នាំថ្មី

Appendix II
Summary of the Cambodian Writing System

Consonants ព្យញ្ជនៈ pjuañ-jiah-nɛa

Here are all the consonants in the Cambodian alphabet listed in alphabetical order. The pronunciation shows whether the consonant is of the /aa/ or /oo/ class.

Consonant	Pronunciation	Sound
ក	gɔɔ	/g/
ខ	kɔɔ	/k/
គ	goo	/g/
ឃ	koo	/k/
ង	ngoo	/ng/
ច	jɔɔ	/j/
ឆ	chɔɔ	/ch/
ជ	joo	/j/
ឈ	choo	/ch/

ញ	ñoo	/ñ/
ដ	dɔɔ	/d/
ប៉	tɔɔ	/t/
ឌ	doo	/d/
ណ	too	/t/
ណា	nɔɔ	/n/
ត	dtɔɔ	/dt/
ថ	tɔɔ	/t/
ទ	dtoo	/dt/
ធ	too	/t/
ន	noo	/n/
ប	bɔɔ	/b/[1]
ផ	pɔɔ	/p/

ព	bpoo	/bp/
ភ	poo	/p/
ម	moo	/m/
យ	yoo	/y/
រ	roo	/r/
ឡ	loo	/l/
វ	vwoo	/vw/
ស	sɔɔ	/s/
ហ	hɔɔ	/h/
ឡ	lɔɔ	/l/
អ	ɔɔ	/ɔɔ/

Note: 1. When sra aa (ា) is added to bɔɔ (ប) the combined new character set becomes បា for *baa*. This is because the normal combination would make the បា character which could be easily confused with the character hɔɔ (ហ). For this reason, an alternate character set was developed. Also, when ប is combined with sra au (ៅ-ៅ) or sra ao (ៅ-ា), it respectively forms បៅ or បៅ in this same manner.

Vowels ស្រៈ sra

These are the twenty-five basic vowel symbols in written Cambodian listed in alphabetical order. The name of each vowel and the sound produced when combined with either /ɔɔ/ or /oo/ series consonants are shown below. If only one sound is shown, that sound should be used for both series of consonants.

Vowel	Vowel Name	Sound /ɔɔ/-/oo/
ា	sra aa	/aa/-/ia/
ិ	sra e	/e/-/i/
ី	sra ey	/ey/-/ii/
ឹ	sra ə	/ə/
ឺ	sra ɨɨ	/ɨɨ/
ុ	sra o	/o/-/u/
ូ	sra oo	/oo/-/uu/
ួ	sra ua	/ua/
ើ	sra aɨ	/aɨ/-/əə/
ឿ	sra ɨa	/ɨa/

ៀ	sra ia	/ia/
េ	sra ee	/ee/
ែ	sra ae	/ae/-/ɛɛ/
ៃ	sra ai	/ai/-/ei/
ោ	sra ao	/ao/-/oo/
ៅ	sra au	/au/-/əʉ/
ុំ	sra om	/om/-/um/
ំ	sra ɔm	/ɔm/-/əm/
ាំ	sra am	/am/-/oam/
ាំង		/ang/-/ɛang/[1]
ះ	sra ah	/ah/-/ɛah/
ិះ	sra eh	/eh/-/ih/[2]

$-\overset{\circ}{\circ}_1$	sra oh	/oh/-/uh/
$\hat{\mathfrak{l}}-\overset{\circ}{\circ}$	sra eh	/eh/-/ih/[2]
$\hat{\mathfrak{l}}-\mathfrak{l}\overset{\circ}{\circ}$	sra ɔh	/ɔh/-/uah/

Note: 1. This vowel is actually not listed as a vowel in the Cambodian alphabet because it is simply *sra am* with a *ngoo* on the end. However, it's distinctive vowel sound convinced us to list it as a seperate vowel.
   2. These two vowels produce identical sounds, but the second one is much more common.

Independent Vowels

Cambodian has eleven more vowel symbols which are called independent vowels. These vowels differ from the other vowels because they stand alone and do not require an accompanying consonant. Therefore, the /ɔɔ/ and /oo/ consonant rules do not apply to these vowels.

Vowel	Vowel Name	Sound
ឥ	sra-ei	/ei/
ឦ	sra-ee	/ee/
ឧ	sra-oo	/oo/
ឩ	sra-ow	/ow/
ឫ	sra-rə	/rə/
ឫ	sra-rʉʉ	/rʉʉ/
ឭ	sra-lə	/lə/
ឮ	sra-lʉʉ	/lʉʉ/

ឯ	sra-ae	/ae/
ៃ	sra-ai	/ai/
ៅ	sra-ao	/ao/

Sub-Consonants ជើង jəəng

These are all the sub-consonants in Cambodian script listed in alphabetical order.

Consonant	Pronunciation	Sound
ក	gɔɔ	/g/
ខ	kɔɔ	/k/
គ	goo	/g/
ឃ	koo	/k/
ង	ngoo	/ng/[1]
ច	jɔɔ	/j/
ឆ	chɔɔ	/ch/
ជ	joo	/j/
ឈ	choo	/ch/
ញ	ñoo	/ñ/[1]
ដ	ñoo	/ñ/[1]
ត	dtɔɔ	/dt/

ฑ	tɔɔ	/t/
ฒ	doo	/d/
ณ	too	/t/
ด	nɔɔ	/n/
ต	tɔɔ	/t/
ถ	dtoo	/dt/
ท	too	/t/
ธ	noo	/n/[1]
น	bɔɔ	/b/
บ	pɔɔ	/p/
ป	bpoo	/bp/
ผ	poo	/p/
ฝ	moo	/m/[1]
พ	yoo	/y/[1]
ฟ	roo	/r/[1]

ល	loo	/l/[1]
វ	vwoo	/vw/[1]
ស	sɔɔ	/s/
ហ	hɔɔ	/h/
អ	ɔɔ	/ɔ/

Note: 1. Unlike other sub-consonants, these sub-consonants follow the consonant class of the uppercase consonant to which they are attached.

Cambodian Punctuation

These are the punctuation marks used in Cambodian writing. Their individual explanations can be found in Chapter 9.

bɔn-dtɔk (បន្ដក់)

tmeeñ gɔn-dao (ធ្មេញកណ្ដុរ)

dtrey-sab (ត្រីសព្ទ)

a-sdaa (អស្ដា)

dton-a-kiat (ទណ្ឌយាត)

ro-baat (របាទ)

sdtuan (ស្ដួន)

sɔm-yook-sañ-ñaa (សំយោគសញ្ញា)

reah mok bpii (រះមុខពីរ)

leek book (លេខប្អូក)

kan (ខ័ណ្ឌ)

៕ល ៕ la nəng la

ៈ sañ-ñaa rial (សញ្ញារៀល)

? sañ-ñaa sɔm-nua
(សញ្ញាសំនួរ)

! (no name)

/ (no name)

Numbers លេខ leek

The last set of characters to learn in the Cambodian alphabet is the Cambodian script for numbers. Normally in Cambodian writing, numbers can either be written through this script or spelled out phonetically. When making larger numbers, these characters are combined just like they are in English.

Consonant	Pronunciation	English
0	soon សូន	0
១	muay មួយ	1
២	bpii ពីរ	2
៣	bey បី	3
៤	buan បួន	4
៥	bpram ប្រាំ	5
៦	bpram-muay ប្រាំមួយ	6
៧	bpram-bpii/bpram-bpəl ប្រាំពីរ	7
៨	bpram-bey ប្រាំបី	8
៩	bpram-buan ប្រាំបួន	9

Consonant Classes

Cambodian script has two classes of consonants: /ɔɔ/ consonants (a-koo-sa) and /oo/ consonants (koo-sa). When combined with a vowel, the class of the consonant affects what vowel sound is rendered because many vowels have one sound for each consonant class.

ក (gɔɔ) + า (aa) = កា (gaa) -- (/ɔɔ/ series consonant

produces the /aa/ sound)

គ (goo) + า (ia) = គា (gia) -- (/oo/ series consonant

produces the /ia/ sound)

Final Consonants

Cambodian script has many different final consonants, some more common than others. Many of these final consonants also change sounds from their normal consonant sound.

Common final consonants:

ក /-k/   ង /-ng/   ញ /-ñ/   ត /-t/
ន /-n/   ប /-b/   ម /-m/   ល /-l/

Less common final consonants:

ខ /-k/   គ /-k/   ដ /-t/   ណ /-n/   ថ /-t/
ឌ /-t/   ជ /-t/   ព /-b/   ភ /-b/

Exception final consonants:

យ /-ii/   ច /-ik/   ឆ /-ik/   រ /-silent/   ស /-h/   វ /-w/

Sub-Consonants

The following words are examples of double consonant sounds in written Cambodian involving lowercase consonants. The character-by-character explanation is presented in the order of the sounds made, not in the order of the written characters. Dashes represent absent consonants. Note that the vowel sound is determined by the class of the sub-consonant.

1. ស្គុម (sgoom) = ស + ុ + ម
$$(s + goo + m)$$

2. ល្ខោន (lkaon) = ល + ្ + ោ + ន
$$(l + k + ao + n)$$

Some sub-consonants are dominated by the class of the attached uppercase consonant. In this case, the vowel sound is determined by the class of the uppercase consonant. Each of these weak sub-consonants are identified in the previous section.

1. ថ្ងៃ (tngai) = ថ + ្ + ៃ- (t + ng + ai)

2. ខ្ញុំ (kñom) = ខ + ្ + ុំ (k + ñ + om)

3. ស្រា (sraa) = ស + ្ + ា (s + r + aa)

Appendix III
Test and Writing Exercise Answers

Test Answers

Test1

Matching:

1. e   2. j   3. b   4. c   5. d
6. g   7. k   8. h   9. a   10. i

Translation:

1. What is your name?
2. Yes, I'm fine.
3. Is this a book or a bag?
4. dtau look sok-sɔb-baay dtee?
5. nih jia gaa-saet, mɛɛn dtee?

Test 2

Matching:

1. g   2. k   3. i   4. a   5. c
6. o   7. f   8. 1   9. b   10. q
11. e   12. h   13. r   14. j   15. m

Translation:

1. The money is in the bag.
2. I have a bed and table.
3. Is he from America or France?
4. dtuu-re-sab nəu ləə dtok.
5. kñom rian pia-saa kmae nəng pia-saa jen.

Test 3

Matching:

1. e   2. m   3. a   4. j   5. o   6. g
7. 1   8. b   9. d   10. k   11. f   12. c

Translation:

1. I know how to write Japanese.
2. May I please go to the bathroom.
3. He wants to go play ball.
4. goat dtəɥ rian nəɥ ban-naa-laay.
5. kñom soom dtəɥ məəl gon baan dtee?

Test 4

Matching:

1. d   2. p   3. b   4. o   5. l   6. q   7. h
8. f   9. a   10. r   11. c   12. j   13. k   14. i

Word Excercise:

1. dəng taa   2. jeh   3. sgoal
4. sgoal   5. dəng taa   6. jeh

Test 5

Telling Time:

1. maong buan (pluɥ)
2. maong bpram-muay (lngiak)
3. maong dɔb-bpii / aa-triat
4. maong bey (ro-sial) haa-seb nia-dtii
5. maong dɔb muay gɔn-lah / maong dɔb muay (bprək) saamseb nia-dtii
6. maong dɔb (yub) sae-seb bpram nia-dtii
7. maong bpram (lngiak) bpram nia-dtii

1. 7:00 p.m.
2. 3:00 a.m.
3. 6:30 a.m.
4. 2:45 p.m.
5. 11:25

6. 12:00 p.m.
7. 4:00 p.m.

Translation:

1. I have been at home since 3:00.
2. He goes to work at 5:00 a.m.
3. Sopha likes to sleep in the morning.
4. tnak rian tɔm jɔb maong buan ro-sial.
5. je-nii gɔm-bpung aan siaw-pəɥ.
6. dtaɥ look jɔng dtəɥ roong-gon jia-muay knia dtee?

Test 6

Matching:

Months
1. h   2. d   3. l   4. a   5. e   6. i
7. c   8. f   9. k   10. b   11. j   12. g

Days
1. c   2. f   3. a   4. g   5. b   6. e   7. d

Translation:

1. I rest from Saturday to Monday.
2. Sometimes, I go to sleep at 12:00.
3. He went to the market in order to buy a book.
4. bpii aa-dtit graoy, kñom dtəɥ srok vwiat-naam.
5. goat (baan) nəɥ nih dtang-bpii maong bpram-muay.

Test 7

Matching:

1. k   2. e   3. g   4. b   5. l   6. i
7. j   8. m   9. h   10. f   11. c   12. d

Translation:

1. I like to eat Cambodian food, but I don't like Vietnamese food.
2. Is Sokha home?
3. When I eat Cambodian food, I use chopsticks.
4. sɔm-lɔɔ nih bprai bpeek.
5. kñom tloab ñam mhoob baa-rang.

Test 8

Matching:

1. d   2. m   3. a   4. j   5. c   6. b
7. i   8. k   9. h   10. e   11. g   12. f

Translation:

1. Is he home yet.
2. I am wearing a white shirt and blue pants.
3. My lower back hurts.
4. kñom dtrəuw-gaa kao-aaw tmey.
5. muak goat tom bpeek.

Test 9

Matching:

A.
1. g   2. a   3. j   4. i   5. h
6. f   7. k   8. c   9. b   10. e

B.
1. e   2. k   3. a   4. j   5. c
6. g   7. i   8. b   9. f   10. d

Test 10

Matching:

A.

1. m   2. e   3. q   4. h   5. a   6. n
7. b   8. l   9. o   10. r   11. c   12. k
13. g   14. p   15. f   16. i

Identification:

1. ming
2. dtaa/om
3. bɔ-oon / oon
4. kmuay
5. bprɛah-ɔng
6. bɔɔng
7. aek-oo-dtɔm
8. look
9. bɔɔng
10. om
11. yiay/om
12. bpaa
13. look
14. bɔ-oon
15. bpuu

Writing Exercise Answers

Writing Exercise 1

1. ខា   2. កេ/កែ   3. ងូ   4. ថិ
5. គូ   6. ង៉ុ   7. កា   8. ជា
9. យី   10. ញ៊ី   11. ឈី/ឈឺ   12. ថី
13. ញា   14. កុ   15. យា   16. ញ៊ី
17. ខុ   18. ឈឺ   19. ងា   20. ជុ

Writing Exercise 2

1. ទា   2. ថា   3. ធា   4. ឈែ
5. ណា   6. ញៀ   7. ធិ   8. តា
9. ថែ   10. ធូ / ជូ   11. ឈ្លៀ   12. ណែ
13. ដែ   14. នើ   15. កុ/គូ   16. ណី
17. ធើ   18. ញា / ញៀ   19. ថែ   20. ទី

Writing Exercise 3

1. ជូប   2. រុំ   3. ឡាន   4. ចាន
5. បឹង   6. នៅ   7. ទិញ   8. ទាំង
9. សម   10. នាង   11. គុល   12. យាយ
13. ចង   14. លា   15. កោត   16. ឈ្យេង
17. ចំ   18. ជូត   19. ជុំ   20. ឈ្យឺន

Writing Exercise 4

1. សាប
2. ឡើយ
3. រះ
4. ហាម
5. ពោះ
6. បោះ
7. អា
8. នេះ
9. ហួស
10. កេះ
11. រ៉ា
12. ដោះ
13. បេះ
14. លះ
15. អាច
16. សែន
17. ជិះ
18. លុះ
19. លាង
20. ហោ

Writing Exercise 5

1. ផ្កា
2. ផ្ទិត
3. ផ្គរ
4. ក្រោះ
5. ក្កាម
6. ម្កាយ
7. ម្ុះ
8. ឡ្ពាន
9. ស្កា
10. ស្គា / ស្គៀ

Writing Exercise 6

1. ផ្សៀង
2. ស្តឹក
3. ស្ូច
4. ច្បារ
5. ស្ី
6. ត្យូង
7. ផ្ទឹល
8. ម្ូប
9. ម្យៅ
10. ស្ូះ

Writing Exercise 7

1. ស្ិត
2. ស្រែក
3. ស្គាក
4. អ្ី
5. ព្យះ
6. ធ្ពេញ
7. ស្យៀក
8. ផ្នែក
9. ព្រោះ
10. ផ្ទើ
11. ព្រែ
12. ស្វែង
13. ក្ុង
14. ប្រធាន

Writing Exercise 8

1. ខ្ញុំ ៣ក់ អារ រងា ខ្សៀវ និង អារ ស

2. គ្រូពេទ្យ មាន ផ្ទះ ធំ

3. ខ្ញុំ ឈឺ ធ្មេញ

4. បង ធិម ត្រូវ គោ ពុកមាត់

5. អ្នក ណា និង សំអាត បន្ទប់ទឹក

Writing Exercise 9

1. ដាក់   2. យ៉ាង   3. ស្ពាតៗ   4. ប្រសាសន៍

5. រាក់ទាក់   6. រង្វាន់   7. ពណិ   8. ធមិ

9. កត់   10. បិច   11. ប៉ុន្ដែ   12. តួចៗ

13. ក៏បាន   14. សង្រួយ   15. មហាវិទ្យាល័យ

INDEX

A

B

C

child	goon	10
China	brɔ-dteeh/srok jen	2
Chinese characters	ak-sɔɔ jen	3
chopsticks	jɔng-gəh	7
city	dtii-grong	10
class	tnak/tnak-rian	3
classifier for a mouthful, words	mat	9
classifier for books and animals	gbaal	9
classifier for bottles	dɔɔb	9
classifier for cans	gɔm-bpong	9
classifier for chunks	dom	9
classifier for documents	jbab	9
classifier for flat things, sheets	sɔn-lək	9
classifier for floors, levels, stories	joan	9
classifier for glasses	gaew	9
classifier for kilograms	gii-loo	9
classifier for kilometers	gii-loo-maet	9
classifier for large bags	baaw	9
classifier for large groups, piles	gəm-noo	9
classifier for machines	gruang	9
classifier for meters	maet	9
classifier for occurances	dɔɔng	9
classifier for objects	daʉm	9
classifier for pairs of things	guu	9
classifier for people	nek	9
classifier for servings of food	jaan	9
classifier for rooms	bɔn-dtob	9
classifier for sets of clothes	gɔm-plee	9
classifier for slices	jɔm-net	9
classifier for small round things	groab	9
classifier for stories, movies	rʉang	9
classifier for strands, threads	sɔɔ-sai	9
classifier for ways, kinds, types	yaang	9
clean	sa-aat	8
to clean	sɔm-aat	8
to clean the house	sɔm-aat pdteah	8
to close, to turn off	bət	10
clothes	kao-aaw/sɔm-liak-bɔm-bpeak	8
coconut	doong	10
cold	trɔ-jeak	9
cold; to have a cold	pdaa-saay	8
college	mo-haa-vwi-dtyia-lay	3
color	bpoa	4
comb hair	set sɔk	8
come	mook	2
come alone	mook mneak-aeng	10
come from	mook bpii	2
computer	gom-bpyuu-dtəə	10
computer technician	jiang-gom-bpyuu-dtəə	10
confused	jrɔɔ-lɔm	10
to cook	tvwəə baay/tvwəə mhoob	7

cool, chilly, cold	ro-ngia	9
to correct	gae	10
country	brɔ-dteeh/srok	2
countryside	srok-srae/jon-ɔ-bɔɔt	10
cow, ox	goo	10
crazy	chguat	10
criminal	oo-grit-ti-jon	10
crocodile	grɔɔ-bpəə	10
cruel, savage	koo-kəʉ	10
cupboard/cabinet	dtuu	10
cylindrical covering	sraom	8

D

daily	bprɔɔ-jam tngai	10
dark	ngo-ngət	9
daughter	goon-srey	10
day	tngai	6
day after tomorrow	kaan-sa-aek	6
day before yesterday	msil-mngai	6
day off; holiday	tngai sɔm-raak	6
December	kae-tnuu/kae-dɔb-bpii	6
deer	chluh	10
dentist	bpeet-tmeen	10
descend	joh	10
dessert	bɔng-aem	7
dictionary	vweah-ja-naa-nu-grɔɔm	2
die	slab	10
die (for animals)	ngoab	10
difficult	bpi-baak	2
diligent	yook-jet-dtuk-dak	9
dirty, soiled	bprɔ-lak	9
dishes	jaan	8
do	tvwəə	3
to do business	rook-sii	10
doctor	bpeet/gruu-bpeet	8
dog	chgae	10
dollar	dol-laa	4
door, opening	dtvwia	2
dry	snguat	9
duck	dtia	10

E

ear	dtrɔ-jiak	8
easy	srual	2
economy, economics	set-a-gik	10
eight	bpram-bey	1
eighty	bpaet-seb	1
elected representative	dtɔm-naang-riah	10
elephant	dɔm-rey	10

embassy	staan-dtuut	3
English language	pia-saa ɔng-glee	2
enough, just right	lmoom	4
evening	bpeel-lngiak/lngiak	5
every	roal	10
excited	rəm-pəəb	10
Excuse me.	ɔt-dtooh	1
exhausted	ɔh-gam-lang	10
expensive	tlai	4
eye	pnɛɛk	8
eyebrow	jeñ-jaʉm	8
eye-glasses	vwaen-dtaa	2
eyelash	room-pnɛɛk	8

F

face	mok	8
fail (a class or test)	tleak	10
fall	tleak	10
family	grua-saa	4
far	chngaay	4
farmer	nek-tvwəə-srae	10
fast	lʉan	4
fat	toat	9
fat stomach	gbaal-bpuah	8
father	oo-bpuk	10
father-in-law	oo-bpuk-kmeek	10
February	kae-gom-peah/kae-bpii	6
feel well	srual-kluan	8
female (for animals)	ñii	10
female, girl, woman	srey	9
fifty	haa-seb	1
final question particle	dtee	1
finger	mriam-dai	8
fingernail	grɔ-jɔɔk (dai)	8
fire; electricity	pləəng	10
fish	dtrey	7,10
fisherman	nek-nee-saat	10
five	bpram	1
flat	riab	9
flower	pgaa	10
food	mhoob, baay	7
food; cooked rice	baay	3
foot	jəəng	8
for	sɔm-rab	7
forty	sae-seb	1
forever, indefinitely	ro-hoot	6
fork	sɔɔm	7
four	buan	1
French food	mhoob baa-rang	7
French language	pia-saa baa-rang	2

Friday	tngai-sok	6
fried rice	baay chaa	7
friend	bpuak-maak	4
from	bpii	2
from, since	bpii/dtang-bpii	5
front	mok	6
fruit	plae-chəə	7
fruit juice	dtək plae-chəə	7
full	ch-aet	7
future tense identifier	nəng	5

G

gas station	haang jak-sang	3
get	baan	3
girlfriend	sɔɔng-saa	10
gloves	sraom-dai	8
go	dtəʉ	3
go on a trip	tvwəə dɔm-naʉ	6
go out, recreate	daʉ-leeng	6
go to sleep	jool geeng	6
goat	bpoo-bpɛɛ	10
good	lɔ-ɔɔ	4
Goodbye.	jəm-riab-lia/lia-sen-haʉy	1
grandfather	dtaa/jii-dtaa	10
grandmother	yiay/jii-doon	10
grass	smau	10
great-grandfather	dtaa-dtuat	10
great-grandmother	yiay-dtuat	10
greater	jiang	9
green	bpoa bai-dtɔɔng	4

H

hair	sɔk	8
half	gɔn-lah	5
hand	dai	8
happy	sɔɔb-baay-jet	10
hard	rəng	4
hat	muak	8
have	mian	2
have ever (done something)	tloab/dael	7
he, she, him, her	goat	2
head	gbaal	8
heart	beh-doong	8
heartbroken	kooik-jet	10
heavy	tngon	9
height	kɔm-bpuah	9
Hello.	jəm-riab-sua	1
hello (on the phone)	aa-loo/jum-riab-sua	7
help	juay	5

horse	seh	10
hospital	mon-dtii-bpeet	3
hot	kdau	9
hour, o'clock	maong	5
house, home	pdtεah	2
housefly	ruy	10
housewife	mee-pdtεah	10
How are you doing?	sok-sɔb-baay dtee	1
how many	bpon-maan	4
how much	bpon-maan	4
hundred	rooy	1
hundred thousand	saen	1
hungry	klian/heew (baay)	7
husband	bdey	10

I

I, me	kñom	1
I don't understand.	min yul dtee	1
I'll see you later.	juab knia tngai graoy (dtiat)	7
I'm sorry.	soom-dtooh	1
important	sɔm-kan	10
in	knong	2
in order to	daʉm-bey	6
in time, on time	dtoan	8
initial question particle	dtaʉ	1
instead, again	vwiñ	1
is, to be	jia/gʉʉ-jia	1
it	vwia	2
It doesn't matter.	min-ey-dtee	1

J

jacket, coat	aaw-ro-ngia	8
January	kae-mak-ga-raaʔkae-muay	6
Japan	brɔ-dteeh/srok jo-bpun	2
job	gaa-ngia-tvəə	10
July	kae-gɔk-ga-daa/kae-bpram-bpəl	6
June	kae-mi-to-naa/kae-bpram-muay	6

K

kitchen	jɔng-graan-baay	7
knee	jong-gong	8
knife	gɔm-bet	7
know	dɔng	4
know how to do something	jeh	3
know of	sgoal	4

L

language	pia-saa	2
Lao, Laotian	liaw	10
last month	kae-mun/kae-gɔn-loong dtəʉ	6
last week	aa-dtit-mun/aa-dtit gɔn-loong dtəʉ	6
later	graoy	6
a later day	tngai-graoy	6
lawyer	mee-tia-vwii	10
lazy	kjil	9
learn, study	rian	2
leave	jeeñ	6
left	chvweeng	2
leg	jəəng	8
lettuce	saa-lat	10
library	ban-naa-lay	3
light	sraal	9
like, prefer	jool-jet	3
lion	dtao	10
lips	bɔɔ-boo-moat	8
listen	sdab	3
a little	bɔn-dtek	7
a little bit	bɔn-dtek-bɔn-dtuiik	3
a little more	bɔn-dtek dtiat	7
live	ruah/ruah-nəʉ	10
liver	tlaʉm	8
lizard	jiing-jɔk	10
long (length)	vwεεng	4
long (time)	yuu	4
lower back; waist	jɔng-geh	8
lung	suat	8

M

magazine	dtuah-sa-naa-vwa-dey	10
male (for animals)	chmool	10
male, boy, man	bproh	9
manager	nek-jat-gaa	10
mango	svwaay	10
many, a lot	jraʉn	4
March	kae-mi-nia/kae-bey	6
market	psaa	3
marry, married	riab-gaa/gaa	10
matter; activity	gek-gaa	10
May	kae-oo-sa-pia/kae-bpram	6
meat	saek	7
mechanic	jiang-maa-siin	10
medication	tnam	8
meet	juab	5
minute	nia-dtii	5

million	lian	1
Monday	tngai-jan	6
money	luy	2
monk	look-sɔɔng	10
monkey	svaa	10
month	kae	4,6
monthly	bprɔɔ-jam kae	10
more	dtiat	5
more	taem dtiat	7
more	jiang	9
morning	bpeel-bprək/bprək	5
mosquito	muuh	10
most, greatest	jiang-gee	9
mostly, majority	piak-jraʉn	10
mother	mdaay	10
mother-in-law	mdaay-kmeek	10
motorcycle	moo-dtoo	7
motorcycle taxi	moo-dtoo-dob	10
mouth	moat	8
movie	gon	3
movie theater	roong-gon	3
moviestar	dtua-aek-gon	10
muscle	saik-dom	8
music	pleeng	3

N

name	chmuah	1
nationality	jun-jiat	10
near	jit	4
neck	gɔɔ	8
need something	dtrʉow-gaa	8
need to do something	dtrʉow	8
new	tmey	8
newspaper	gaa-saet	1
next month	kae-graoy	6
next week	aa-dtit-graoy	6
Nice to meet you.		
	kñom sɔb-baay-jet baan juab look	1
niece or nephew	kmuay	10
night	bpeel-yub/yub	5
nine	bpram-buan	1
ninety	gau-seb	1
no	dtee/ɔt-dtee	1
no, not, do not	min/ɔt	1
No problem.	min-ey-dtee	1
normal	tom-mdaa	6
nose	jrɔ-muh	8
not feel well	min-srual-kluan	8
not in time	min-dtoan	8
not so...	min sʉow	7

not tasty	min/ɔt chngaañ	7
not the same	min dooik-knia	9
not yet	nəu lauy	8
November	kae-vwi-ji-gaa/kae-dɔb-muay	6
nowadays	sɔb-tngai nih	10

O

October	kae-dto-laa/kae-dɔb	6
okay, all right	gɔ-baan	7
old	jah	8
older brother	bɔɔng-bproh	10
older cousin	bɔɔng-jii-doon-muay	10
older sibling	bɔɔng	10
older sister	bɔɔng-srey	10
oldest sibling	goon-bɔɔng-gee	10
on, above	ləə	2
one	muay	1
one moment	muay-pleet	7
One moment please.		
	soom jam muay-pleet	7
oneself	aeng	10
one-tenth of a riel	gak	4
only	dtae	9
only (final particle)	dtae-bpon-nɔh	9
open, to turn on	baʉk	10
or	rʉʉ	1
orange	grooik	10
orange juice, soda	dtək krooik	7
over here	nəu nih	2
over there	nəu nuh	2
over there (farther)	nəu nɔh	2

P

palm fruit	tnaot	10
pants	kaaw	8
paper	krɔ-dah	2
park	jɔɔt	10
possession particle	ro-bɔh	10
pass	joab	10
past tense identifier	baan	5
past, already occured	gɔn-loong	6
pedicab	sii-kloo	7
peel	jet	7
pen	bik	1
pencil	kmau-dai	1
phone number	leek dtuu-re-sab	4
picture; photograph	ruub/ruub-tɔɔt	2
pig	jruk	10
place	dtii/dtii-gɔn-laeng/gɔn-laeng	10

place	dak	10
plant, grow	dam	10
play	leeng	3
please	soom	3
plural particle	dteang	9
police	bpoo-lih/dɔɔm-ruat	10
politics	noo-yoo-baay	10
poor, impoverished	grɔɔ	9
poor, inadequate	ɔn	9
pork	saik-jruuk	7
possible	baan	3
post office	brai-sa-nii/bpoh	3
present tense identifier	gɔm-bpung	5
president	bprɔə-tian	10
pretty, beautiful	sa-aat	8
problem	bpɔñ-ña-haa	8
profession, occupation	aa-jiib	10
province	kaet	10
pure	sot	7
purified or bottled water		
dtək sot/dtək bɔɔ-ri-sot		7
put	dak	10

Q

quality	guna-piab	10
question particle	dtau	1

R

radio	vwi-dtyu	10
rambutan	saaw-maaw	10
read	aan	3
Really?	mɛɛn?	1
red	bpoa grɔ-hɔɔm	4
refrigerator, freezer	dtuu-dtək-gɔɔk	10
regularly	jia-bprɔɔ-jam	10
remember	jam	7
remove	dɔh	8
rest	sɔm-raak	6
restaurant	poo-ja-niiy-taan	3
rice	baay	7
rice (unmilled)	srɔuw	10
ride	jih	7
riel (Cambodian currency)	rial	4
right	sdam	2
Right?	mɛɛn dtee?	1
right now	ee-luow (nih)	10
right, correct	mɛɛn	1
ring	jiñ-jiang	8
rise	laung	10

road, path	plɔuw	4
Roman alphabet		
ak-sɔɔ ɔng-gleeh/ɔk-sɔɔ baa-rang		3
room	bɔn-dtob	2
run	rot	10

S

sad, troubled	bpi-baak-jet	10
salty	bprai	7
same	dooik-knia	9
Saturday	tngai-sau	6
school	saa-laa/saa-laa-rian	3
second	vwi-nia-dtii	5
secretary	lee-kaa	10
see	kəəñ	10
September	kae-gañ-yaa/kae-bpram-buan	6
seven	bpram-bpii/bpram-bpəl	1
seventy	jet-seb	1
shade	mlob	10
shave	gao	8
sheep	jiam	10
shirt	aaw	8
shoes	sbaek-jəəng	8
short	dtiab	9
short	kley	4
shoulder	smaa	8
siblings, family	bɔɔng-ba-oon	10
sick; to hurt	chuu	8
similar	dooik	9
single	liiw	10
sit	ɔng-guy	10
sit down	ɔng-guy joh	10
six	bpram-muay	1
sixty	hok-seb	1
skilled worker	jiang	10
skin	sbaek	8
skinny	sgoom	9
skirt	sɔm-bpot	8
sleep	geeng/deek	3
sleepy	ngo-nguy-geeng	10
slow	yuut	4
small	dtooik	4
small percentage, minority	piak-dtek	10
snake	bpuah	10
So, (what about...?)	joh	1
soap	saa-buu	8
soccer	bal-dtoat	3
socks	sraom-jəəng	8
soft	dton	4
some	klah	3

sometimes	juan-gaal	6	thick	grah	9
son	goon-bproh	10	thigh	pləʉ	8
soup	sɔm-lɔɔ/sub	7	thin	sdaʉng	9
sour	juu	7	think	git	6
speak	ni-yiay	3	thirty	saam-seb	1
spicy	həl	7	this	nih	1
spoon	slaab-bpria	7	this coming April		
sports, athletics	gey-laa/bal	3	kae-mee-saa kaang 'mok nih		6
stand	choo	10	this one	aa-nih	4
stand up	choo laʉng	10	thousand	bpoan	1
start, begin	jab-pdaʉm	5	three	bey	1
state	roat	2	three days	bey tngai	6
station	staa-nii	3	three months	bey kae	6
stir fry	chaa	7	three months ago		
stomach	bpuah/grɔ-bpeah	8	bey-kae-mun/bey-kae-gɔn-lɔɔng dtəʉ		6
stop	chob	10	three months from now	bey kae graoy	6
store	haang/psaa	3	through, by means of	daoy	10
strong	klang	9	Thursday	tngai-bpra-hoa	6
student	ni-set/goon-səh	10	tiger	klaa 10	
Sunday	tngai-aa-dtit	6	time	bpeel/vwee-lia	5
sweet	pa-aem	7	to ask (for something)	som	7
			to bathe	muik-dtək	8

T

			to be alive	nəʉ-ruah	10
			to be diligent	yook-jet-dtuk-dak	9
T-shirt	aaw-yʉʉt	8	to be fine	sok-sɔb-baay	1
table	dtok	2	to be something	tvwəə-jia	10
tailor, seamstress	jiang-gat-dee	10	to brush teeth	doh tmeeñ	8
take	yook	4	to buy	dtiñ	3
take off clothing	dɔh kaaw-aaw	8	to clean	sɔm-aat	8
take off shoes	dɔh sbaek-jəəng	8	to clean the house	sɔm-aat pdteah	8
tall; high	kbpuah	9	to close, to turn off	bət	10
tap water	dtək maa-siin	7	to comb hair	set sɔk	8
tasty, delicious	chngaañ	7	to come	mook	2
teacher (female)	nek-gruu	10	to come alone	mook mneak-aeng	10
teacher (male)	look-gruu	10	to cook	tvwəə baay/tvwəə mhoob	7
teeth	tmeeñ	8	to correct	gae	10
telephone	dtuu-re-sab	2	to descend	joh	10
television	dtuu-rə-dtuah	3	to die	slab	10
ten	dɔb	1	to die (for animals)	ngoab	10
ten thousand	mʉʉn	1	to do business; make a living	rook-sii	10
test, exam	bprɔ-lɔɔng	10	to do; to make	tvwəə	3
Thai alphabet	ak-sɔɔ tai	3	today	tngai-nih	6
Thai food	mhoob tai	7	toe	mriam-jəəng	8
Thailand	brɔ-dteeh/srok tai	2	together	knia	5
Thank you.	ɔɔ-gun	1	tomato	bpeeng-bpɔh	10
that	nuh	1	tomorrow	sa-aek/tngai-sa-aek	6
that	taa	4	too (as in "too much")	bpeek	4
that one	aa-nuh	4	too much, too many	jraʉn bpeek	7
the big one	aa-tom	4	too...	bpeek 7	
the small one	aa-dtooik	4	tourism	dteeh-sɔ-jɔɔ	10
they, them	gee/puak gee	2	tourist	dteeh-sɔ-jɔɔ	10

trader	nek-lok-doo	10
train	ro-dteh-pləəng	3,10
train station	staa-nii ro-dteh-pləəng	3
translate, interpret	bɔɔk-bprae	10
translator, interpreter	nek-bɔɔk-bprae	10
tree	daʉm-chəə	10
trip	dɔm-naʉ	6
T-shirt	aaw-yʉʉt	8
Tuesday	tngai-ɔng-gia	6
twenty	mpei	1
two	bpii	1
two days	bpii tngai	6
two months	bpii kae	6
two weeks from now	bpii aa-dtit graoy	6

U

uncle	bpuu	10
under	graom	2
understand	yul	1
Understand?	yul dtee	1
university	saa-kɔɔl-vwi-dtyia-lay	3
unlike, dissimilar	min dooik	9
until	ro-hoot dɔl	6
use	bpraʉ	7
usually	tom-mdaa	6

V

vegetables	bɔn-lae	7
vendor	nek-lok	10
very, much	nah	2,4
Vietnam	brɔ-dteeh/srok viat-naam	2
village	puum	10
visit, vacation	dtəʉ-leeng	6
volleyball	bal-dteah	3

W

wake up	graok-laʉng	6
walk	daʉ	4
want	jɔng	3
wash	liang	8
wash clothes	baok-kao-aaw	8
wash dishes	liang jaan	8
wash your hair	gɔk sɔk	8
watch	məəl	3
watch, clock	nia-le-gaa	1
water	dtək saab	7
water buffalo	grɔɔ-bey	10
water; fluid	dtək	7

way, direction	kaang	2
we, us	yəəng/yəəng kñom	2
weak	ksaoy	9
wealthy, rich	mian	9
wear	sliak-bpeak	8
wear pants or a skirt	sliak	8
wear something (above the waistline)		
	bpeak	8
Wednesday	tngai-bput	6
week	aa-dtit/sa-bdaa	6
weight	dtom-ngon	9
wet	dto-dtək/saʉm	9
what	a-vwey	1
What time is it?	maong-bpon-maan (haʉy)	5
when (future)	ɔng-gaal	5
when (past)	bpii-ɔng-gaal	5
where	nəʉ (ae) naa	2
which day	tngai naa	6
which month	kae naa	6
which one	muay naa	4
which; where	naa	2
white	bpoa sɔɔ	4
who	nek naa	4
why	haet a-vwey	7
wife	bprɔɔ-bpon	10
window	bɔɔng-uik	2
with	jia-muay	5
wolf	chgae-jɔ-jɔɔk	10
work	tvwəə-gaa	3
write	sɔɔ-see	3

Y

year	chnam	4,6
yearly	bprɔɔ-jam chnam	10
yellow	bpoa lʉang	4
yes (female speaker)	jaa	1
yes (male speaker)	baat	1
yesterday	msil-miñ	6
yet	haʉy-rʉʉ-nəʉ	8
you	(see pages 229-230)	10
you; person	nek	1
younger brother	bɔ-oon-bproh	10
younger cousin	bɔ-oon-jii-doon-muay	10
younger sibling	bɔ-oon	10
younger sister	bɔ-oon-srey	10
youngest sibling	goon-bpəʉ	10

About the Authors

Richard Kent Gilbert is a Cambodian language linguist who has been studying and using the Cambodian language ever since he served as a Cambodian language missionary for The Church of Jesus Christ of Latter-day Saints. Upon the completion of his missionary service, he continued his education and graduated from Brigham Young University with a B.A. in International Politics. In 2001, Mr. Gilbert also worked as an intern for the United States Agency for International Development at the United States Embassy in Phnom Penh, Cambodia. He still keeps in close contact with the Cambodian community in both Cambodia and the United States. Mr. Gilbert currently resides in the San Francisco Bay Area and works as a freelance Cambodian language translator and interpreter. Most of his work is as a registered Cambodian language court interpreter for the State of California.

Sovandy Hang was born in Phnom Penh, the capital of Cambodia. He arrived in the United States of America as a refugee in June 1982. He lived in Oklahoma City with his family for six months before they moved to Oakland, California. Sovandy graduated from Cal State University with a Bachelor's degree in Business Administration. He enjoys working with low-income families and at-risk young people. He is actively involved in the Cambodian community and has extensive experience translating school newsletters, brochures, flyers, and official documents. He has taught Cambodian youth to read and write Cambodian at a nearby community center. Now Sovandy works as a child welfare social worker and provides on-going translation and interpretation services to his fellow Cambodians in the San Jose and Oakland areas. He also serves as a substitute teacher for the Cambodian School of San Jose, California.

Titles from Paiboon Publishing

Title: **Thai for Beginners**
Author: Benjawan Poomsan Becker ©1995
Description: Designed for either self-study or classroom use. Teaches all four language skills- speaking, listening (when used in conjunction with the cassette tapes), reading and writing. Offers clear, easy, step-by-step instruction building on what has been previously learned. Used by many Thai temples and institutes in America and Thailand. Cassettes & CD available. Paperback. 270 pages. 6" x 8.5"

| Book | US$12.95 | Stock # 1001B |
| Two CDs | US$20.00 | Stock # 1001CD |

Title: **Thai for Travelers** (Pocket Book Version)
Author: Benjawan Poomsan Becker ©2006
Description: The best Thai phrase book you can find. It contains thousands of useful words and phrases for travelers in many situations. The phrases are practical and up-to-date and can be used instantly. The CD that accompanies the book will help you improve your pronunciation and expedite your Thai language learning. You will be able to speak Thai in no time! Full version on mobile phones and PocketPC also available at www.vervata.com.

Book & CD   US$15.00   Stock # 1022BCD

Title: **Thai for Intermediate Learners**
Author: Benjawan Poomsan Becker ©1998
Description: The continuation of Thai for Beginners . Users are expected to be able to read basic Thai language. There is transliteration when new words are introduced. Teaches reading, writing and speaking at a higher level. Keeps students interested with cultural facts about Thailand. Helps expand your Thai vocabulary in a systematic way. Paperback. 220 pages. 6" x 8.5"

| Book | US$12.95 | Stock # 1002B |
| Two CDs | US$15.00 | Stock # 1002CD |

Title: **Thai for Advanced Readers**
Author: Benjawan Poomsan Becker ©2000
Description: A book that helps students practice reading Thai at an advanced level. It contains reading exercises, short essays, newspaper articles, cultural and historical facts about Thailand and miscellaneous information about the Thai language. Students need to be able to read basic Thai. Paperback. 210 pages. 6" x 8.5"

| Book | US$12.95 | Stock # 1003B |
| Two CDs | US$15.00 | Stock # 1003CD |

Title: **Thai-English, English-Thai Dictionary for Non-Thai Speakers**
Author: Benjawan Poomsan Becker ©2002
Description: Designed to help English speakers communicate in Thai. It is equally useful for those who can read the Thai alphabet and those who can't. Most Thai-English dictionaries either use Thai script exclusively for the Thai entries (making them difficult for westerners to use) or use only phonetic transliteration (making it impossible to look up a word in Thai script). This dictionary solves these problems. You will find most of the vocabulary you are likely to need in everyday life, including basic, cultural, political and scientific terms. Paperback. 658 pages. 4.1" x 5.6"
Book   US$15.00 Stock # 1008B

Title: **Improving Your Thai Pronunciation**
Author: Benjawan Poomsan Becker ©2003
Description: Designed to help foreigers maximize their potential in pronouncing Thai words and enhance their Thai listening and speaking skills. Students will find that they have more confidence in speaking the language and can make themselves understood better. The book and the CDs are made to be used in combination. The course is straight forward, easy to follow and compact. Paperback. 48 pages. 5" x 7.5" + One-hour CD
Book & CD   US$15.00 Stock # 1011BCD

Title: **Thai for Lovers**
Author: Nit & Jack Ajee ©1999
Description: An ideal book for lovers. A short cut to romantic communication in Thailand. There are useful sentences with their Thai translations throughout the book. You won't find any Thai language book more fun and user-friendly. Rated R!
Paperback. 190 pages. 6" x 8.5"
Book   US$13.95 Stock #: 1004B
Two CDs   US$17.00 Stock #: 1004CD

Title: **Thai for Gay Tourists**
Author: Saksit Pakdeesiam ©2001
Description: The ultimate language guide for gay and bisexual men visiting Thailand. Lots of gay oriented language, culture, commentaries and other information. Instant sentences for convenient use by gay visitors. Fun and sexy. The best way to communicate with your Thai gay friends and partners! Rated R!
Paperback. 220 pages. 6" x 8.5"
Book   US$13.95 Stock # 1007B
Two Tape Set   US$17.00 Stock # 1007T

Title: **Thailand Fever**
Authors: Chris Pirazzi and Vitida Vasant ©2005
Description: A road map for Thai-Western relationships.   The must-have relationship guidebook which lets each of you finally express complex issues of both cultures.   Thailand Fever is an astonishing, one-of-a-kind, bilingual expose of the cultural secrets that are the key to a smooth Thai-Western relationship. Paperback. 258 pages.   6" x 8.5"
Book   US$15.95 Stock # 1017B

Title: **Thai-English, English-Thai Software Dictionary
           for Palm OS PDAs With Search-by-Sound**
Authors: Benjawan Poomsan Becker and Chris Pirazzi ©2003
Description: This software dictionary provides instant access to 21,000 English, Phonetic and Thai Palm OS PDA with large, clear fonts and everyday vocabulary. If you're not familiar with the Thai alphabet, you can also look up Thai words by their sounds. Perfect for the casual traveller or the dedicated Thai learner. Must have a Palm OS PDA and access to the Internet in order to use this product.
Book & CD-ROM US$39.95 Stock # 1013BCD-ROM

Title: **Thai for Beginners Software**
Authors: Benjawan Poomsan Becker and Dominique Mayrand ©2004
Description: Best Thai language software available in the market! Designed especially for non-romanized written Thai to help you to rapidly improve your listening and reading skills! Over 3,000 recordings of both male and female voices. The content is similar to the book Thai for Beginners, but with interactive exercises and much more instantly useful words and phrases. Multiple easy-to-read font styles and sizes.   Super-crisp enhanced text with romanized transliteration which can be turned on or off for all items.
Book & CD-ROM US$40.00 Stock # 1016BCD-ROM

Title: **Lao-English, English-Lao Dictionary for Non-Lao Speakers**
Authors: Benjawan Poomsan Becker & Khamphan Mingbuapha ©2003
Description: Designed to help English speakers communicate in Lao. This practical dictionary is useful both in Laos and in Northeast Thailand. Students can use it without having to learn the Lao alphabet.   However, there is a comprehensive introduction to the Lao writing system and pronunciation. The transliteration system is the same as that used in Paiboon Publishing's other books. It contains most of the vocabulary used in everyday life, including basic, cultural, political and scientific terms. Paperback. 780 pages. 4.1" x 5.6"
Book   US$15.00 Stock # 1010B

Title: **Lao for Beginners**
Authors: Buasawan Simmala and Benjawan Poomsan Becker ©2003
Description: Designed for either self-study or classroom use. Teaches all four language skills- speaking, listening (when used in conjunction with the audio), reading and writing. Offers clear, easy, step-by-step instruction building on what has been previously learned. Paperback. 292 pages. 6" x 8.5"
Book   US$12.95 Stock # 1012B
Three CDs   US$20.00 Stock # 1012CD

Title: **Cambodian for Beginners**
Authors: Richard K. Gilbert and Sovandy Hang ©2004
Description: Designed for either self-study or classroom use. Teaches all four language skills- speaking, listening (when used in conjunction with the CDs), reading and writing. Offers clear, easy, step-by-step instruction building on what has been previously learned. Paperback. 290 pages. 6" x 8.5"
Book   US$12.95 Stock # 1015B
Three CDs   US$20.00 Stock # 1015CD

Title: **Burmese for Beginners**
Author: Gene Mesher ©2006
Description: Designed for either self-study or classroom use. Teaches all four language skills- speaking, listening (when used in conjunction with the CDs), reading and writing. Offers clear, easy, step-by-step instruction building on what has been previously learned. Paperback. 320 pages. 6" x 8.5"
Book   US$12.95 Stock # 1019B
Three CDs   US$20.00 Stock # 1019CD

Title: **Vietnamese for Beginners**
Authors: Jake Catlett and Huong Nguyen ©2006
Description: Designed for either self-study or classroom use. Teaches all four language skills- speaking, listening (when used in conjunction with the CDs), reading and writing. Offers clear, easy, step-by-step instruction building on what has been previously learned. Paperback. 292 pages. 6" x 8.5"
Book   US$12.95 Stock # 1020B
Three CDs   US$20.00 Stock # 1020CD

Title: **Tai Go No Kiso**
Author: Benjawan Poomsan Becker ©2002
Description: Thai for Japanese speakers. Japanese version of Thai for Beginners. Paperback. 262 pages. 6" x 8.5"
Book   US$12.95 Stock # 1009B
Three Tape Set   US$20.00 Stock # 1009T

Title: **Thai fuer Anfaenger**
Author: Benjawan Poomsan Becker ©2000
Description: Thai for German speakers. German version of Thai for Beginners. Paperback. 245 pages. 6" x 8.5"
Book   US$13.95   Stock # 1005B
Two CDs   US$20.00   Stock # 1005CD

Title: **Practical Thai Conversation DVD Volume 1**
Author: Benjawan Poomsan Becker ©2005
Description: This new media for learning Thai comes with a booklet and a DVD. You will enjoy watching and listening to this program and learn the Thai language in a way you have never done before. Use it on your TV, desktop or laptop. The course is straight forward, easy to follow and compact. A must-have for all Thai learners! DVD and Paperback, 65 pages 4.8" x 7.1"
Book & DVD   US$15.00   Stock # 1018BDVD

Title: **Practical Thai Conversation DVD Volume 2**
Author: Benjawan Poomsan Becker ©2006
Description: Designed for intermediate Thai learners! This new media for learning Thai comes with a booklet and a DVD. You will enjoy watching and listening to this program and learn the Thai language in a way you have never done before. Use it on your TV, desktop or laptop. The course is straight forward, easy to follow and compact. DVD and Paperback, 60 pages 4.8" x 7.1"
Book & DVD   US$15.00   Stock # 1021BDVD

Title: **A Chameleon's Tale - True Stories of a Global Refugee -**
Author: Mohezin Tejani ©2006
Description: A heart touching real life story of Mo Tejani, a global refugee who spends thirty four years searching five continents for a country he could call home. Enjoy the ride through numerous countries in Asia, Africa, North and South America. His adventurous stories are unique – distinctly different from other travelers' tales. Recommended item from Paiboon Publishing for avid readers worldwide. Paperback. 257 pages. 5" x 7.5"
Book   US$19.95   Stock #1024B

Title: **Thai Touch**
Author: Richard Rubacher ©2006
Description: The good and the bad of the Land of Smiles are told with a comic touch. The book focuses on the spiritual and mystical side of the magical kingdom as well as its dark side. The good and the bad are told with a comic touch. The Sex Baron, the Naughty & Nice Massage Parlors, the "Bangkok haircut" and Bar Girls & the Pendulum are contrasted with tales of the Thai Forrest Gump, the Spiritual Banker of Thailand and the 72-year old woman whose breasts spout miracle milk. Paperback. 220 pages. 5" x 7.5"
Book   US$19.95   Stock #1024B

Title: **How to Buy Land and Build a House in Thailand**
Author: Philip Bryce ©2006
Description: This book contains essential information for anyone contemplating buying or leasing land and building a house in Thailand. Subjects covered: land ownership options, land titles, taxes, permits, lawyers, architects and builders. Also includes English/Thai building words and phrases and common Thai building techniques. Learn how to build your dream house in Thailand that is well made, structurally sound and nicely finished. Paperback. 6" x 8.5"

Book   US$19.95   Stock #1025B

Title: **Retiring in Thailand**
Authors: Philip Bryce and Sunisa Wongdee Terlecky ©2006
Description: A very useful guide for those who are interested in retiring in Thailand. It contains critical information for retirees, such as how to get a retirement visa, banking, health care, renting and buying property, everyday life issues and other important retirement factors. It also lists Thailand's top retirement locations. It's a must for anyone considering living the good life in the Land of Smiles. 6" x 8.5"
Book   US$19.95   Stock #1026B

Coming Soon in 2007

- **Lao for Travelers** by Saikham Jamison
- **Vietnamese for Travelers** by Jake Catlett
- **Cambodian for Travelers** by Richard Gilbert
- **Burmese for Travelers** by Gene Mesher
- **Paragon English Vol. 1** A textbook for Thai people to learn English

Title: **Living Thai**
-Your Guide to Contemporary Thai Expressions- Vol. 1
Author: Benjawan Poomsan Becker ©2007
Description: This series of books and CDs is a collection of numerous words and expressions used by modern Thai speakers. It will help you to understand colloquial Thai and to express yourself naturally. You will not find these phases in any textbooks. It's a language course that all Thai learners have been waiting for. Impress your Thai friends with the real spoken Thai. Lots of fun. Good for students of all levels.

Title: **Thai Law for Foreigners**
Author: Ruengsak Thongkaew ©2007
Description: Thai law made easy for foreigners. This unique book includes information regarding immigration, family, property, civil and criminal law used in Thailand. Very useful for both visitors and those who live in Thailand. Written by an experienced Thai trial lawyer. It contains both the Thai text and full English translation.

Title: **The Smart Medical Tourist**
Authors: Julie Munro and Hari DePietro ©2007
Description: A unique guide book for travelers looking for medical treatment that is affordable, safe, stress-free, with the most advanced medical technology and world class medical providers. This well researched book from medical tourism insiders includes the history, development and economics of medical tourism, stories of medical travelers for both cosmetic surgery and specialized surgery including heart and orthopedic procedures, how to choose a doctor, planning ahead, comparing costs, getting medical and travel insurance, and much more. Covers Thailand, Singapore, Malaysia, India, Dubai, South Africa, Brazil, Mexico, Costa Rica, and other countries.

Title: **How to Establish a Successful Business in Thailand**
Author: Philip Wylie ©2007
Description: This is the perfect book for anyone thinking of starting or buying a business in Thailand. This book will save readers lots of headaches, time and money. This guide is full of information on how to run a business in Thailand including practical tips by successful foreign business people from different trades, such as guest house, bar trade, e-commerce, export and restaurant. This is an essential guide for all foreigners thinking of doing business - or improving their business - in Thailand.

PAIBOON PUBLISHING
ORDER FORM

QTY.	ITEM NO.	NAME OF ITEM	ITEM PRICE	TOTAL

Delivery Charges for First Class and Airmail

	USA and Canada	Other Countries
Up to $25.00	US$3.95	US$8.95
$25.01-$50.00	US$4.95	US$11.95
$50.01-$75.00	US$6.25	US$15.25
$75.01-$100.00	US$7.75	US$18.75
Over $100.00	FREE	US$18.75

Merchandise Total _____

CA residents add 8.25% sales tax _____

Delivery Charge (See Chart at Left) _____

Total _____

Method of Payment ❑ Check   ❑ Money Order   Make payable to Paiboon Publishing

Charge to: ❑ Visa   ❑ Master Card   ❑ Amex

Card # _____   Exp. Date _____/_____

Signature_____ Tel _____

Name _____ Date _____

Address _____

_____

_____

Email Address _____

Mail order is for orders outside of Thailand only.
Send your order and payment to: Paiboon Publishing
PMB 192, 1442A Walnut Street, Berkeley, CA 94709 USA
Tel: 1-510-848-7086 Fax: 1-510-848-4521
Email: paiboon@thailao.com Website: www.thailao.com
Allow 2-3 weeks for delivery.

PAIBOON

PUBLISHING